Generations to Come

Becoming All Things to Your Child

By Dale Sadler

Dale Sadler

Licensed Professional Counselor

Mental Health Service Provider

Dale Sadler earned his Bible degree from Freed-Hardeman University and his master's degree in Marriage and Family Therapy from Western Kentucky University. He is currently a School Counselor at Portland East Middle School, and is also in private practice as a family counselor in White House, TN. Dale also serves as the part-time youth minister for the Birdwell's Chapel Church of Christ in Cottontown, TN. He has served as youth minister for the Portland and Union Hill Churches of Christ (five and four years respectively). Dale and his wife Malita live in White House with their two children. He grew up in Carthage, TN where he attended the Carthage Church of Christ.

www.Dale

dale@dales

D1291547

ISBN: 978-0-89098-624-0

©2014 by 21st Century Christian
2809 12th Ave S, Nashville, TN 37204
All rights reserved.

All rights reserved. No part of this publication may be reproduced, stored in a retrieval system, or transmitted in any form or by any means—electronic, mechanical, photocopy, recording, digital, or otherwise—without the written permission of the publisher.

Unless otherwise noted Scripture quotations are from the New American Standard Bible.
Scripture taken from the NEW AMERICAN STANDARD BIBLE®,
Copyright © 1960,1962,1963,1968,1971,1972,1973,1975,1977,1995 by The Lockman Foundation.
Used by permission.

Unless otherwise noted Scripture quotations are from the English Standard Version.
Scripture quotations are from The Holy Bible, English Standard Version® (ESV®),
copyright © 2001 by Crossway, a publishing ministry of Good News Publishers.
Used by permission. All rights reserved.

DEDICATED

For Mom and Dad

ACKNOWLEDGEMENTS

This book has been on my hard drive for a long time. It started as a blog and eventually became a Bible study at the Birdwell's Church of Christ in Cottontown, TN where my family worships and I serve as the youth minister. It was during this time that I fully developed the model, mentor, and guide philosophy. I am thankful to those friends/parents, young and old, who were patient with me as I worked to establish my material while growing and learning as a parent along with them. The support of this good congregation to those in need and on their spiritual path continues to amaze me.

I am so thankful to my wife, Malita for enabling me to work on this book while she handled more than her share of the household responsibilities. This is just one example of how she has been supportive of me as I pursued my dream of a private practice and being an author. She continues to amaze me with her patience and dedication to our family. Without her, I wouldn't be the man I am today. She is a fabulous mother, a wonderful Christian example and the love of my life.

It is always good to hear people encourage you from the sidelines and I have lots to thank for this. My friend Matthew Morine has been an encouragement and guide to me along this journey. My mom, dad, and sister have always cheered me on even when I thought the task was impossible.

To those ministers, professors, and other friends who have been there for me, thank you.

TABLE OF CONTENTS

FOREWORD

Malachi 4:6 was the last word of revelation for roughly five hundred years. It is the closing verse of the Old Testament, and it doesn't lose its opportunity to be powerful and memorable.

"...he will turn the hearts of fathers to their children and the hearts of children to their fathers."

The family was God's idea and He knows how important families are. Anyone who has stood in front of an audience with an open Bible has felt that if they could affect the families in that audience, if they could help them see God's principles of parenting, it would do more to affect the eternity of their children and their children's friends than any one thing.

My wife and I raised two boys and our greatest delight is that they love the Lord. Yet, so very often I wished for backup—for more good, solid, reliable information to aid in my parenting. Sometimes just for conformation. Sometimes to help me move through and properly apply the biblical text to our context.

From the first few paragraphs Dale Sadler had my attention front and center. As a minister I see, almost daily, adults behaving in ways that are potentially destroying their children's chances at healthy lives, attitudes, and Christ-likeness. He says: "If you don't like what you see in your child, the first place you need to look is inward." That statement IS this book in a sentence.

I certainly wish I'd had this book as a young parent and can assure you I'll be giving one to the parents of my grandchildren. This is as good a work on proactive parenting as I have seen. It is a cold splash in the face against passive parenting. Wisdom flows all though this book. It will "parent" the parents and mentor the mentors.

As teacher, minister, counselor, and parent Dale has treaded where angels durst not! Telling us how to raise our kids—but listen, weigh, consider prayerfully the approaches and practices he advocates.

Right at the halfway point in this book he says: "We have one chance to raise our children." This is true. Let's make the most of it. To the glory of our Lord and the salvation of our children.

Blessings,
Dale Jenkins
Evangelist/Pulpit Minister Spring Meadows Church of Christ
Co-founder of TheJenkinsInstitute.com

INTRODUCTION

To state the painfully obvious, being a parent is frustrating. Gone are the days of a simple spanking for every infraction your child commits. Today, we try other ways to be effective and, while I am happy about this, it complicates things. With this desire to do more for our children comes the daunting task of knowing what to do, how to do it, when to do it, and to what degree. While parenting has changed, children have not.

Some parents have been blessed with a little angel that does everything he is asked. Other parents however are raising a child that seems to always be defiant. She doesn't listen and only does what she wants. The conflicts grow until the only thing mom and dad know is that they are trying to keep chaos at bay one moment at a time. They cannot enjoy their child and do not have the faintest idea of what that means. If mom and dad don't do something, they will never gain control of their child in order to teach and raise her as God intended. Instead, she will be left to the consequences of her own mistakes.

My passion for families began in Dr. Cravens' Marriage and Family class at Freed-Hardeman University. He started every class with a Far Side cartoon that in one way or another related to the family. This illustrated to me how "far out" some families can be, because the humor was often painfully true. It might have been a grizzly bear ignoring his son who wanted attention, but it was a father all the same. Wives nagging their inattentive husbands and children left to their own devices were all comedic windows into the real chaos some families live in each day.

I wrote this book for a few reasons. First, through my own learning about the subject of parenting, I have garnered a great deal of information that most people have no idea exists. I do not think I have all the answers, but I do have a passion for parenting because becoming one changed me more quickly than anything else I've ever experienced. Even becoming the husband my wife deserves has been a slow metamorphosis. Parenting is still changing me, and even though I have yet to raise a teenager, I have worked with thousands of them at the middle school where I have been a counselor since 2004 and in various ministry capacities for twenty years.

Another reason I wrote this book is because I have a passion for marriage. In counseling couples one of the conflicts that comes up repeatedly is, of course, parenting. Many couples get stuck on parenting and while they are arguing over how to insure their little one's self-esteem isn't scarred, their marriage is crumbling.

This book is what I want to tell struggling parents who cry in my office. I also want to help parents who know what to do, but can't find the strength to carry it out. Parenting is tough and, hopefully, you can find the strength you need to be what your child needs.

I hope my work brings you closer to your child, your spouse, and ultimately your Savior because our heavenly Father is our perfect parenting example.... By the way, His children disobey Him too.

God bless,
Dale

PART 1 - MODEL

CHAPTER 1

Model the Adult
You Want Your Child to Be

"I'm worried about my mom. She said last night that she just wanted to 'end it all.'" Gary tells me this, and for the first time in my career, I have to work to save someone who is not in the room with me. Gary's mother had been sleeping in her car for a few days. Being in and out of work, she wanted to take her own life. After reaching her on her cell phone, I was able to give her the number for the Crisis Hotline in our area. Gary told me a few days later that his mother had received help and was doing better.

William cries in my office, horrified that his dad will punish him for making a B on his report card. "Dad almost didn't pass. Why does he expect me to do any better? He hates reading, but wants me to do it every night." William is expressing a typical familial struggle, that of academics and the incongruence of his dad's expectations and his own past performance.

Kevin, tired of being without power in his house for two weeks, finally begins telling me what's going on at home. His step-dad *won't* work, and his mother is doing all she can to raise her children. He's a gifted student. He is good at making everyone think that things are OK at home even though he rarely eats and is lacking in a lot of support areas; but he is making it.

Children struggle at school with their friends and grades, but many struggle at home as well. These struggles consist of parents who are inconsistent or whose lifestyle sets them up for difficulty with their children. "My little children, let us not love in word, neither in tongue; but in deed and in truth" (1 John 3:18). Some parents forget this and try to lead a life different than what they are admonishing their children to lead. On the other hand, parents are human and have made mistakes that they don't want their own children to make. In either case, the model side of parenting is crucial if your child is to be anything of the positive sort.

Parents can often be heard saying, "Do as I say, not as I do." These parents, deep down wanting their children to make good decisions, tell their children what to do but live a totally different life themselves. This incongruent struggle can cause a lot of turmoil in the home. Parents who live noticeably different than they admonish their children to live are setting themselves up for difficulty to say the least. A former principal friend of mine tells the story about a parent who calls to tell why her child won't be coming in to school. "He's sick and won't be making it today," was her excuse. "Oh really," the principal said, "Well, he just walked in, so I guess he's feeling much better." Don't expect your child to be honest if you are not honest yourself. Expect them to lie to you especially. You want your child to eat healthy? You better put down the doughnut. You want your child to respect authority? Then, civility is the name of the game when speaking to his teachers. If you don't like what you see in your child, the first place you need to look is inward.

The first several years of life are the most impressionable. Your child sees you as the example of adulthood. They will model that in their own child-like way. If daddy hits mommy, that must be the thing to do. If mommy has a shopping addiction, that must be how adults handle their troubles. Our coping skills, behaviors, and bad habits are seen by our children daily. If you want them to be an admirable adult, you must do the same. I wanted my son to stop biting his finger nails. Well, guess what I had to do? I don't want my son to be a couch potato, so it is on the exercise bike I go. If you are happy with your life now, will you be happy with such a life being exhibited by your children?

The Model

This study is about helping parents be better parents. Most books help the parent understand their child as this one does. However, parental actions that are separate from molding a child will not work. Parental actions must revolve around developing a child into who you want him or her to be. Your son or daughter is the direct result of everything you have done or not done for them.

The model is everything parents do when they think the child is not looking. It is what you do when you think your child is asleep or too young to understand. It is the home life you develop with your spouse (the actors) while your child (the audience) sits and watches. It is probably your biggest tool that is the most difficult to use. Why? It brings the demons in your life front and center with who you are trying to get your child to become. All your aspirations for your child sit firmly on who you are as a model.

Titus 2:2-8 (NASB) gives some good advice for all of us raising a family

> "Older men are to be temperate, dignified, sensible, sound in faith, in love, in perseverance. Older women likewise are to be reverent in their behavior, not malicious gossips nor enslaved to much wine, teaching what is good, so that they may encourage the young women to love their husbands, to love their children, to be sensible, pure, workers at home, kind, being subject to their own husbands, so that the word of God will not be dishonored. Likewise urge the young men to be sensible; in all things show yourself to be an example of good deeds, with purity in doctrine, dignified, sound in speech which is beyond reproach, so that the opponent will be put to shame, having nothing bad to say about us."

We know what these things mean. "Well, I teach reverence and how not to gossip. I teach that getting drunk is bad. Sure." You teach these things, but do you live them? What does your life teach? The life you lived as a teen and the life you are trying to live now? What is your narrative? Is it one where you rose from a difficult childhood into a successful career? Are you from a home that was full of advantages and now you cannot handle struggles? Where are you in your life now as your child looks to you as the example of how he or she is supposed to be?

When I Was Your Age

There's another issue at play—that of parents who planted and reaped their wild oats as children and are working to make sure their child doesn't make the same mistakes.

One card teens will try to play is, "Didn't you do this when you were my age?" What is a parent supposed to say? How much do you tell your child about your past? This "self-disclosure" comes up in counseling. If a client is facing a similar situation that you have encountered, how much should you, the counselor, share in regards to your experience? If the counselor is looking for pity, admiration, or (help us all) guidance from the client, the counselor should not disclose said event. However, if the intent is to show the client your success despite the obstacles or to make a connection in order to reach the person better, then it is a good decision to share what happened to you. If you believe your child wants to use the information against you, be careful.

You don't want this to backfire.

Proverbs 1:8-9 (ESV) says, "Hear, my son, your father's instruction and forsake not your mother's teaching, for they are a graceful garland for your head and pendants for your neck." Where do you think the instruction and teaching you have to give originates? It comes a great deal from your own experiences. Don't make excuses for your actions and don't minimize what you did. However, you do want to be honest. Show them your regret for what you did and do not simply tell them a better way, but help them see it.

Let's say you do open that rusty door of half-forgotten indiscretions. "You're a hypocrite," your 16 year-old may say, and, well, she'd be wrong. If you smoked now and wanted her to stop, she could use that word, but if it's been 10 years since, then she should listen to your wisdom based on experience. Crying "hypocrite" can be a distraction to the real issue at hand and furnish a reason for your daughter to yell at you some more and make you feel bad so she can go about her business. Samuel Johnson (1709-1784) was a philosopher and author who defined hypocrisy as:

> Nothing is more unjust, however common, than to charge with hypocrisy him that expresses zeal for those virtues which he neglects to practice; since he may be sincerely convinced of the advantages of conquering his passions, without having yet obtained the victory, as a man may be confident of the advantages of a voyage, or a journey, without having courage or industry to undertake it, and may honestly recommend to others, those attempts which he neglects himself.

An overweight doctor is not wrong if he tells you that you need to lose weight. A marriage therapist who has been divorced three times might not know how to apply her concepts to her own life, but she can help you understand the truths that have saved lots of other marriages. A child will argue *ad hominem* in order to falsify a parent, but this argument is not enough. You must admit your faults, but continue with the premise that even though your past might be wrong, your present logic is correct.

Despite this new relief for parents everywhere, a good example is still the best way to live one's life for one's children. Your past may be questionable, but to expect your child to filter out your actions from your hour-long lectures is impossible. They will not be able to surpass you in virtue and character unless the base you give is solid. You might not have been the teen you wish for them to be now, but you can portray the traits you hope they model in order to be the adult you want someday.

Little boys and little girls need parents who will fulfill their God-ordained roles. Whether by immaturity or simply a lack of understanding, men and women often don't succeed in being the adult their child can appreciate. Men who lie and women who become vindictive within the family system are not helping their kids develop. Many adults need to become just that . . . adults.

King of the Cul-de-Sac

Men want to be dominant in something. We want to feel and believe that we are king of our realm. The desire is not to be obeyed as a king, but to lead effectively and be admired and loved by our family for our abilities. Like Tarzan and other heroes, we want to save the girl, protect our loved ones, and be viewed as a positive force for those who depend on us. So, why don't more men do this? I would submit that they don't know how. Many men are confused about their role. They have a desire to be the man they see on TV, but many are smart enough to know that the womanizing, beer-guzzling behavior doesn't get them very far. Furthermore, behaviors labeled as "manly" are often demonized, and the man who could be a solid force in his own home is ostracized, leaving his daughter without a daddy and his son without a role model of manhood. We must be men, doing what our hearts dictate, but a goal must be balanced with being the father your children need.

A problem arises when men are gone all the time. For those who hunt and fish a lot, part of this desire comes from how things were done before we picked up our food packaged and frozen. Men shot something, threw it over their shoulder, and took it home to cook over a fire that they built. Now that's manly. Nothing is challenging about pushing a buggy through a grocery store no matter how congested the aisle is. For those who work unreasonably often, this is how they take care of their family. This is what they do. It is possible to be physically gone a lot, but still emotionally attached to your children.

All this sounds very positive, but it does have an ugly side. Men may engage in behaviors that ensure their absenteeism because they are afraid to face the fact that they don't measure up in some areas. Instead of trying and possibly failing, some men do what they understand and avoid the rest, even if loving sons need them. In addition to this elusiveness, some men strive to do the minimum because they don't have to risk anything. This is safe, but if nothing is risked then nothing is lost except maybe one's manhood.

Dominance over one's self and the trials at home cannot be attained this way. In Disney's animated adaptation of Tarzan, he climbed a lot of trees before killing the jaguar. You must start somewhere, too.

What do you want to care for in your life? What is it in your life that you want to lead? I hope it is your family; your wife and your children. These are the most fulfilling, albeit difficult, to master. You may have to risk a little or you may have to look yourself in the eye if you fail, but stop hiding and stop making excuses. Satan prowls about as a lion in our world today. You have inside you an inner hunter, so keep the bad things out.

Being a Man's Man

Frank Hopkins was a long-distance horse rider born shortly after the Civil War. He became popular in America by winning over 400 races. His fame soon spread overseas to Arabia where a 3,000-mile race across the desert started with 100 horses but finished with only five. Frank won on his horse Hidalgo, thirty-three hours ahead of the second place finisher.

This story is a testament to the American spirit, but it also shows what a man should be about. Hard work, grit, and tenacity are some of our greatest tools. Too many boys are left to figure out manhood on their own, and too many "men" are still trying to figure it out. In a world where we are expected to be tough yet sensitive, how should a man act?

First, a man should take care of his business with his family. Paul tells the Corinthian husbands to fulfill their duty to their wives. He then continues the chapter with a discussion of sex and, as most husbands know, fulfilling a wife's sexual expectations starts way before you enter the bedroom. Apparently the Corinthian families were having difficulty with this issue. Sex will often take care of itself when all other areas of a marriage (communication, leisure time, etc.) are going well.

Second, a man should be honest with his family so that they know who he is. Too many men lead a double life; that can't be done forever. Affairs and apathetic spouses lead to a home that no one would want to be a part of. Both spouses are often guilty of taking for granted what they have at home. So, men, be honest about your family. What can you do to make it better?

Men should be honest with themselves, too. It took Nathan's story to get David to see his sin with Bathsheba. David, going against sound judgment, made several bad choices. David thought he was safe. Like men of today, David may have excused his behavior. He may have justified it. "I'm the king."

Be honest with yourself, and be a model for your son. Be a model for your daughter's future husband.

All of the items mentioned above take a tough man to carry them out. The movie based on Frank Hopkins' life shows a man who had shortcomings. He drank a lot and seemed perpetually miserable at the start of the movie. Once he agreed to the Arabian race, he found purpose again and straightened out his life. If you have made a commitment to your family, carry it out at whatever place you might be in life. It will make you stronger as a man, and you'll be forced to be honest, a trait that just might turn you into someone your children can be proud to call Daddy.

On television, and in life, men seem to get beat up a lot in the home. For some, they deserve it, but for others, not so much. Even though we tend to blame men for failed marriages and families, the women have a great part in this as well.

Mothers Can Be Too Motherly

Characteristics inherent in women that make them great mothers can also be their downfall and their children's. Meg Meeker, in her book *Strong Fathers, Strong Daughters*, discusses the issue of women and their need to understand. I like understanding, but it can cloud the issue at hand. I have experienced this concern with moms I talk to at school. They want to know why their boy wants to start fires. For some reason, "because he's a boy" isn't good enough. Understanding is good, but when it comes to children, what difference does it make? I want my son to pick up his toys. If he will not do this when I ask him, wondering, "why, why, why?" will not do me any good. What matters is that he does what I ask. The question of "Why" is irrelevant.

Mothers are typically given the "nurturer" label. My son and I box with these very large inflatable gloves. We have a blast. Then, when he gets hurt, he cries and wants his mama. The bad side to this is when mothers feel the need to nurture and coddle way beyond what is developmentally appropriate, which can vary from child to child. My wife and son are very close. He has always been good to do what we ask him and has always been very independent. However, in beginning pre-school, it was a struggle for us to leave him. Pulling him out and saving him felt like the right thing to do, but he has to start school sometime and that time is now. Seventh grade boys can brush their own hair, eighth grade boys can get their own stuff together for school, and freshmen boys can cut up their own steak. Finishing a daughter's thoughts, not letting her speak, and picking her friends are also traits where a mother's need to guide her child bleeds into the realm of control and dampening her child's development. Children must experience and do things at certain ages in order to grow into the adult they are destined to become. If a mother (or father) steps in too often in the name of love and nurturing, the plan to help the child actually backfires.

Many women were once little girls dreaming of their Prince Charming. Although women of today are strong and self-reliant, they also enjoy being pursued by a gentleman caller. The ultimate hope is that our daughter will find a man who will provide a family and a strong support system both for her and for her future children. This desire can also get very ugly. Why does a woman leave a drunk only to find herself in the exact same situation? Why does a woman leave a good paying job, two cars, and a home to live with a man who must beg for help each week from local services? This answer goes very deep as it considers the woman and her desire for a life. It can also be very simple though if one considers what the woman has done and what she is currently doing. Women who seem to make poor relationship decisions do so because, in what they pursue, they hope they will find fulfillment.

You Have What It Takes

A man must be the best man he can be for his family and a woman must be the best mother she can be. With the two together, there is a synergy that is unmatched. A strong home will have its problems, but if it is truly strong, it will overcome any difficulty and thus send children into the world with strong beliefs and values that can carry them through life.

For the single mom or the dad struggling with any number of issues, these ideas may seem difficult. They are difficult even for the most well-adapted American couple raising 2.5 kids. You must ask, "What is the struggle coming from?" Because you hear your own parents and understand how traumatic the experience was, so you have determined to do nothing that might hurt your child, including discipline? Are you currently making decisions that hinder you as a parent? They might not be wrong necessarily, but unless your daily actions make you a better parent, they are probably slowing you down in that arena. Part of being an adult is knowing what you believe and what you want. This is the only way you will pass your values on to your children, which is the core issue. Strife in your home should come from your child not wanting to do. It is your job as the model; as the parent to show him or her. Strife should not (although it mostly does) come from your child attempting to tell you what to do and challenging your actions. As we end this section of the book, remember to be the model your child can respect. Although you have made mistakes, one you do not want to make is leaving your child behind and faced with the task of finding his or her own way in life.

Questions for Discussion

1. How does the phrase, "do as I say, not as I do" resonate with you as a parent? Is it a barrier to your parenting?

2. How does the portrayal of men and women in today's society affect your parenting?

3. What are your children's beliefs about how boys (and girls) should act?

CHAPTER 2

The Model Within
Your Family System

Your Family's System

Are you thirty-six years old and you still get treated like the youngest sibling? Are you twenty-four and you still sit at the kiddie table during Christmas dinner? Times do not seem to change when it comes to families. Also, do you speak with your friends about how different your second child is from your first? The stories all seem the same. The first child was easier, and the second needs to lay off the caffeine. What is to account for these issues?

Your family is a system, and it does not change much as you grow older. This is why your older cousin still speaks to you the way she did when you were teenagers. Usually major life events curb this behavior. Going off to college and starting families will often remake a family as the members mature. This is not always the case though because some families are resistant to a change in their structure, especially if the forty-year-old uncle still thinks he is eighteen.

Why is your second child so different from your first? You might not have thought of this, but your second child is actually born into a different type of family than his or her older counterpart. Your first was born with germ-fighting non-child adults. Your second was born into a family where you wiped the dirty pacifier on your pants before giving it back.

Virginia Satir compared the family system to a hanging mobile in a baby's crib. In a mobile, pieces of different sizes and shapes can be grouped together in such a way to balance simply by changing the distance between the parts. Family members, like parts of a mobile, require certain things in order to remain balanced. When something changes, like distance between family members, disequilibrium occurs and manifests itself through emotional upheaval and stress. The family may adapt to this new set up, or it may try to restore balance by forcing the "errant" member to return to old positions.

As a system, your family acts in ways that work. Everyone's behavior is affected by all those in the household, which can make for a pleasant or chaotic home life depending on the circumstances. A working family system may mean, in a positive sense, that Dad makes the coffee and Mom cooks breakfast. Morning tasks are completed, and everyone benefits. This working system can also be negative. Maybe Mom covers up for Dad's drinking habit. This works because it completes the desired result of secrecy, but it is obviously unhealthy. Dad's problem may be spiraling out of control, but Mom works to protect him.

Family systems theory is often referenced when working with addicts. Despite the chaos within a family with a drug addict or alcoholic as a member, they continue to function, but to the detriment of the members. Peggy Ferguson, Licensed Marriage and Family Therapist, says it this way, "The addict's relationship to the chemical contributes to the family pathology. As the addict becomes more and more disabled by addiction, family members adapt to accommodate the changes in the addict." In other words, it is easier to maintain balance and do what the addict wants, than to confront the issue. This is an extreme example, but indicates how families are systems.

A dysfunctional family can be defined as a unit that does not adapt to the growing and changing needs of its members that are necessary for full self-actualization. In other words, if your family is dysfunctional, the members may not develop as they should. If the mother gets a great deal of satisfaction from raising a baby and doting over him or her, she may continue certain practices that keep the five-year-old boy in a state of dependency. He should be learning independence, but instead his maternal dependence continues. This came to the forefront of discussion with the May 2012 *Time* magazine cover that pictured a mother breast-feeding her then six-year-old son. Some would not label this dysfunctional, but others would as it is perpetuating a behavior that is not necessary for survival. It keeps a young boy needlessly dependent on his mother.

This "attachment parenting" (also called enmeshment) can continue even into adulthood. A child can depend on a parent or even a sibling to do things for him. Why should a two-year-old ask for something when older sister always gets him what he needs? Why should a middle schooler learn to clean his room when Mom always does it for him? Why should a teenager learn to do his homework when Dad does it all the time? Why should a married woman depend on her husband when she knows her dad will give her all she wants?

This pattern of behavior can also be seen in the twenty-something age bracket as more and more young adults continue to live at home. Referred to as the "Boomerang Generation," college graduates are moving back in with their parents as a result of difficult economic times, but also because it is simply easier to do. Faced with a desire to start economically where their parents left them at age 18 but with salaries that cannot possibly provide that, boomerang adults would rather live at home. Boys who love their video games and get sexual fulfillment from pornography and casual relationships have less of a desire to start a family. Women have less of a need to get married because they can often make it by themselves, particularly if Mom and Dad are paying the rent.

When the system is healthy, things are great. They are not perfect, but the family members benefit and grow through difficult and fun times. However, if the system is unhealthy, something must change and this change can be met with great opposition as one or more members try to get out of a system they view as unbearable. This can often throw families into a whirlwind, but unless you address the problem, it may never get better.

Dysfunction Within the Home

One account in Scripture shows exactly how a family can "function" in such a way that it works to get the members what they want even though the method drove the family members to division. In Genesis 25 we read about Jacob and Esau. To be clear, I make no attempt to question their family dynamic in regards to how God utilized them to accomplish His will. However, their differences, jealousy, and the family conflict that ensued are all proof that man and families have not changed much. Although many try to blame technology, the schools or even a child's peers, what it comes down to is this: how our children relate to one another and the world around them is much more about how they grow up in their family system.

Jacob was the favorite of his mother, but Esau was loved by his father (Genesis 25:27-28). Certainly, there can be a natural gravitation between child and parent based on interests and other similarities. If the relationship your spouse has with your child is divisive, if you are jealous and want to see them fail, this is a recipe for disaster within your family unit. It certainly was within Isaac and Rebekah.

Genesis 27 brings the story to its climax by illustrating the deception possible in the family. Rebekah helped Jacob receive his father's blessing when it actually belonged to Esau. How many families are in similar states? The husband and wife are at odds with each other and use the children, money, or even the threat of divorce as game pieces. The child cannot grow up effectively because one or both parents are impeding this growth. Maintaining a healthy home is not entirely about what you think you are doing: being a part of a church, going to scouts or sports; but rather it is about what you are doing every moment of every day.

John Lennon said that life is what happens to you when you are making other plans. Your child had a big Christmas, she takes three different kinds of lessons, and she has all of the best clothes. Who cares? Does she know you love her and does she know that her mom and dad love each other? My wife and I make it a habit of grossing out our kids with PDA. We love each other, and you should love your spouse as well.

In the case of Isaac, Rebekah and Jacob, we read of a common familial pattern known as triangulation. Rebekah wanted Jacob to have the blessing, and, no doubt, he wanted it too. In desiring what was rightfully Esau's, Rebekah and Jacob pitted themselves against Esau. Here again, I am not questioning God's wisdom, but simply wish to illustrate how family patterns of function have not changed.

Think of this in today's terms. Your son wants a toy. He asks Dad who says no. He then sprints to Mom's side, crying for the item and Mom caves, reprimanding Dad for saying no. Or in the case of a teenage daughter who wants to go out with some friends. Dad thinks it is OK, but mom does not, and an argument ensues because they are not on the same page. Triangulation, divide and conquer, call it what you want, the child is manipulating the parents to get what he or she wants. This is often an indication of the parents not being together in parenting; their most important job, second only to maintaining their marriage and raising godly children.

Roles Within the Family System

Children

In the book, *Forgiving Our Parents*, Dwight Lee Wolter describes the various roles played by children in dysfunctional homes; homes that are riddled with alcoholism, drug addiction, or any number of abusive situations. Even without these extreme characteristics, children can assume these various roles because it is either how they are treated or it brings about a pleasurable result in their young minds.

The Good Child (aka the Hero): This child acts like the parent to younger siblings or even the parents themselves. He works hard to get good grades, brings home extra money, or is the only one in the home actually succeeding. He is the one the parents compare the other children to. "Why can't you be more like your big brother?" This child can also thrive on attention and have a perfection complex. In dysfunctional situations, anxiety may even manifest itself through Obsessive Compulsive Disorder. This behavior works to maintain a level of control in family situations that are out of control.

The Problem Child or Rebel (aka the Scapegoat): This child is blamed for things that happen within the home. Even when he is not really a part of the actual problem, he may choose to act out in order to stop various dysfunctions from occurring. For instance, he may break something to stop Mom and Dad's arguments. If he is in trouble, the other bad stuff is not happening. In his mind, control is maintained while all attention is placed on his behavior and the other, more serious problems are not addressed. For him, this is a relief. In therapy, this child may actually be brought in as the identified patient (IP).

The Caretaker: This child carries a great burden as he or she believes the dysfunction is her fault or that she can somehow fix what is going on. This is a serious issue in that a child is trying to deal with what is often an adult problem, and wants desperately to fix what is going on, but does not have the resources to do so.

The Lost Child: There is so much going on within the home, this child is often overlooked. He does not get in to trouble, but because this one is not a part of the actual arguing or negative dynamic, his or her needs are overshadowed by the child or children who demand so much more attention. This child would like to be seen, but his parent's behavior tells him that there are more pressing needs and his can wait.

The Mascot: Like the scapegoat, this child tries to get attention placed on him to distract everyone from what is actually going on. When an argument takes place, he works to get attention, distracting everyone from the real problem.

The Mastermind: This child capitalizes on the other family members' faults to get whatever he or she wants. If he acts scared and hurt after an argument between Mom and Dad, he may play this part toward Mom in order to get extra dessert or a new toy. If one of the parents feels a failing somehow in their role as parent, they will placate this negative feeling with the good feeling of giving in to the child's wish. This is wrong for obvious reasons in regard to materialism, but what is not so obvious particularly for the parent involved, is that good parenting is replaced with a pattern of bad "make-the-child-feel-good" parenting.

In each of these cases, the children are acting only in ways that work for them. They have mastered a role and work to maintain order, bear the burden, or fix things as they believe it can be done. In reality, these roles maintain dysfunction in homes where the parents not only have a serious addiction (alcohol, drugs), but also where the atmosphere in the home is somehow chaotic.

These roles manifesting themselves are particularly true with the parents who do not have a clear vision for their children. There is a problem in the home (a cheating spouse, constant arguing, extended family issues) and the child assumes a task to fit into this system. He or she is manipulating and being manipulated in order to function. An elephant is in the room, and no one talks about it. They go about their daily tasks, do not communicate with others, and hope no one tries to communicate with them.

Buried Dysfunction

Although your family may not be dysfunctional because of addiction, your home can function in a way that keeps the family members from growing effectively. The wording of 1 Corinthians 13 works well here.

> If I sit at the dinner table without conversing with my son, am I having an effect on him?

> If I attend all my son's ballgames, but do not know his friends, am I really involved in his life?

> If I allow my daughter to dress immodestly and simply pray that she remain sexually pure, am I guarding her as I should?

> If I allow my seven-year-old to dictate all his activities, am I really helping him to grow as God would intend?

This buried dysfunction keeps you from really joining with your children and your spouse. It keeps you from enjoying your family as God intends. You receive fulfillment from your work, from reading books you enjoy, and from eating, but do you receive fulfillment when spending time with your family? If not, a level of animosity begins to grow that can drive family members apart. If you are not enjoying your time together as a family, something must change.

Do you enjoy speaking with your family? You may say, "yes, we talk," but discussing the events of the moment such as ball practice, what's for dinner, and why the siblings constantly fight are not enriching at all. They do not solidify family ties and are simply base level discussions to handle the moment. Wonder why your teen does not talk to you? It is probably because you have never done it before. Telling you about how much homework she has is not the same as discussing her views on premarital sex, which by the way, had better be a regular part of your discourse.

It has been said that parents spend just seven minutes a day talking to their children. Why? This is the result of Time Monopolization. You spend so much time doing your own thing that you spend no time doing family things. Family time, discussion time with your kids, must be made. It must be purposeful.

You must put ideas in your children's heads that you want them to remember. You must make memories. You must change what your child does if he is doing something you do not like. Do not ask if your son would rather throw ball than play video games. His answer will be, "No." Over time, if you have not made time to influence your child, there will be Polarization. This occurs when one member of the family sees something differently than another member of the family. The values within the system are being challenged. This can be healthy as your son questions what he has been taught and then sees God's truth shining through. This will be the true testament to your parenting. Someday when you are sitting with your child, if his values reflect what you have taught him, then Proverbs 22:6 will ring true. "Train up a child in the way he should go, even when he is old he will not depart from it."

Mom and Dad's Roles

With the knowledge of various roles our children play in the home, how do you as a parent participate in this dance? First, you can be a *Disengaged* parent. This parent is often the one who sees the child only on weekends because of divorce. This parent works to maintain a "fun time" with Mom/Dad persona. He or she does not want to upset the child because they spend so little time together anyway and because it is just easier. Like grandparents who send home a spoiled child, this non-custodial parent can be a non-participant in practical upbringing. Furthermore, with parents in a divorced situation, it is particularly easy for the child to pit the two together such as in triangulation. If at least one parent does not see the child's behavior for what it is, then the mastermind can win.

A parent can also be a *Supporter* of the child's negative behavior, helping to maintain the dysfunctional role of the child. The child's actions often reward this parent somehow. For instance, good graces of the child may be secured with the mother who believes everything the "Good Child" says. Her allegiance is more to her offspring than to her husband. This cannot work as it drives a wedge between Mom and Dad rather than establishing within their unit a tone of cohesion that works to raise the child. Another example may look like this: the parent retreats to her child when hurt by someone at work or even within the home (husband, another child, or an extended family member). The "Caretaker" would then work to be there for the mother in a way that is inappropriate when the child is not yet of a mature age.

Confused: Something is wrong but is not sure what it is. This parent is dealing with another parent who is one of the above. At a loss of options, he/she remains on the sidelines and watches as time after time opportunities are missed to help the child and the spouse have a better relationship. This can be devastating to a marriage as the parent supporting the child's negative behavior sees the other parent as the enemy. A worried mom or dad should seek professional help at this point and get on the same page with one another because nothing can secure a child's future like two parents working for the same outcome: a well-adjusted child.

When we bring children into this world we do so with the expectation that they are going to be great kids, and we are going to be great parents. Then, reality happens, and our vision of a family is soon wrecked because it is more difficult than we thought. To remedy this, parents will work to make their children happy. If you are using this as your sign of parenting success, you are sadly mistaken. It is not our job as parents to make our children happy. Happiness should be a by-product of good parenting where responsibility, self-denial, and empathy are taught in your home. These truly make for happy and healthy human beings.

Functioning as a System

This entire book is about functioning better as parents in order to optimize your family system. There will be difficult times in even the best of families.

So how can you tell if you are on the right path?

First, are you doing what is best for your family in light of God's instructions? Parenting decisions are often made by what is the easiest thing to do in the moment. Worn out from a day at work, parents have little energy to control and monitor their children. This is unfortunate, but it is what we signed up for. What are your values? If you asked your child what is most important to your family, what would he/she say? This came up during our preacher's lesson one Sunday, and it scared me. What would my son say? When we got in the car, my wife asked him. He said, family and God. Hopefully, we are doing something right.

Second, in the moment of interaction with your child, who is in control? When my son was two and three years old, he loved Thomas the Train. Bookstores like Barnes and Noble would have a Thomas the Train table set up in the kids' area, and he would go directly to it every time we visited. This train table was the proving ground for parental control. Would the child behave with other children his age? When it was time to go, would the child fight the parent? Who is really in control? There are children whose personalities make them difficult to control. Some children are easier going than others. However, does your child do what you say? At the end of the day, who has won the battle for your child's mind, you or Satan?

Third, what is important that your child learn? In one large swoop, parents work to teach their child everything they are ever to learn. While at church, they expect their two-year-old to sit quietly on the pew, sing, pray, give, and listen. A greater task to place on a child does not exist. Remember, he is a child and will be resistant to some of these things sometimes just because you are asking him. In worship, as in life, the best way to teach is that of modeling. You are stacking the deck against yourself if you ask of your child a level of maturity that he or she may not be ready for. What is important for a two-year-old to learn in worship? Be quiet. This is still difficult for some as my daughter announces to everyone as she goes potty.

Teaching them to be quiet first is good because it is about the only thing they can really do and it is something they need to do. Can your child do more? Then require that, but back off if things do not progress or if they do not seem to be working. Parents put undue pressure on themselves and their children when they expect beyond what the child is capable of doing.

Conclusion

Families function in ways that work. The questions we should consider are there: "Is your family working for the betterment of all involved?" "Are you instilling responsibility, dependence and a love for God through the values in your home?" There will be mistakes, but if you can hug your child and love your spouse at the end of every day, you are functioning well.

Questions for Discussion

1. In what ways does your family function positively as a system?

2. Consider what negative things are happening in your family. How are you contributing to that negative dynamic?

3. How can members of the family triangulate one another?

CHAPTER 3

Model
Your Marriage

Don't Stay Together for the Kids

It's no surprise that the institution of marriage is in turmoil. Couples, at their marital breaking point, often choose divorce as a solution. I know that divorce is not always avoidable, and many have scriptural reasons for it. However, research is quite clear on children of divorce and the struggles they face. Your chances of divorce increase with each subsequent marriage. Therefore, if you simply take your problems from your first marriage to your second, what have you actually accomplished? We must work on what we have before us rather than trading it in. The grass might be greener, but you still have to mow it.

Divorce, under almost any circumstance, can be traumatic. Emotional devastation, added burdens, and the uncertainty of it all can send each spouse into a whirlwind, taking months or even years to recover. The children also suffer from divorce. Not to be misunderstood, many single parent and step-family homes do a wonderful job with their children because of healthy modeling of what a family can be. Whatever your family looks like, it must be a positive place for sons and daughters to learn their roles as spouses and parents.

One problem with many marriages is that one or both spouses are not completely committed. Love is not a hole you fall into, yet some treat it that way. Couples who were once passionate are now stagnant because things like money, work and even children have skewed their perspective. These daily life tasks absorb their energy and drive them to the point that they have little to give the kids and even less to give to each other. Love must be nurtured over time as each partner changes and develops as a person.

Robert Fulghum, author of *Everything I Need To Know I Learned In*

Kindergarten, tells the story of a culture that believes when couples argue they are making love. In this scenario you come to a better understanding and appreciation of one another as the conflict is resolved constructively. You are "making" love.

Some couples argue without resolution; and instead of growing together, they grow apart. The controversy must end positively for both parties; otherwise it will fester, and the gloves will come out each time the subject is revisited.

Many couples, not wanting to hurt their children through divorce, stay together. This is terribly short-sighted. Spouses who do not work on what is killing their relationship will only give their children a framework of what an unhealthy marriage looks like. "Sweep it under the rug and everything will be fine." How awful! You must do more than stay together. You must work on your marriage for your children and for yourselves.

Why Get Married?

Over the last 60 years, the home has changed a great deal. We are currently moving into a generation of parents who grew up having many peers with divorced parents or even unwed parents. The women in these relationships have grown up in a world much different than that of their mothers and grandmothers. These women have grown up with a choice either to marry or not. Unlike earlier generations, they are not confined to the kitchen, but rather have the option of living on their own or being half of a two-income family. Despite these changes, many women and men still continue to see the benefits of marrying and of raising a family as God intended. The modern world with all its supposed answers to the family unit cannot come up with a better situation than a man and a woman who both love each other and who work to raise godly children.

The statistics build a strong case for marriage, thereby solidifying what God has been telling us all along. According to Scott Haltzman, MD, author of *The Secrets of Happy Families: Eight Keys to Building a Lifetime of Connection and Contentment*, "Ninety percent of married women who were alive at age 45 make it to 65. This is compared to only a little more than 80 percent of divorced and never-married women." Mortality rates are 50 percent higher for unmarried women.

The news is even better for men. Those who were alive at 48 years old also "had a 90 percent chance of reaching age 65 if they were married, but only a 60 to 70 percent chance if they were single—that's a 250 percent higher mortality rate."

According to EverydayHealth.com, there are other reasons to get and stay married:

- A divorced man can expect to have the same life expectancy as that of a man who is married and smokes.
- Unmarried people spend twice as much time in hospitals as married people.
- Cancer cures are 8 to 17 percent more successful when a patient is married; research showed being married was comparable to being in an age category 10 years younger.
- Divorce or marital separation more than doubles the risk of suicide in men.
- Tying the knot results in a decreased risk for substance abuse. Married men and women drink less alcohol and use less marijuana and cocaine than those who are not married.
- Divorced men are more likely to smoke, while married men are likely to quit.
- Seventy percent of chronic drinkers were divorced or separated, while only 15 percent were married.

Haltzman says that "Marital status was the most important factor for predicting depression. Rates of major depression were nine times higher in unmarried men." Depression and in particular dysphoria—a feeling of anxiety, depression, and unease—were also higher in single women compared to married women.

The benefits of a good, healthy marriage are clear, but what does this actually look like or not look like?

Choosing Misery

With the obligations put on us by society, our family, our church, and even our own conscience, actually cultivating a good marriage can be quite difficult. We can choose whether or not we have a good marriage. The concept of choosing our situations has greatly diminished over the years as people are more inclined to be victims than the writers of their own life. Believe it or not, some people choose a miserable co-existence with their spouse and are little more than roommates who discuss bills and share responsibilities within the home. Why would someone choose to be miserable?

Marriage is about letting another person fully into your life, but when we are not happy with ourselves, we work to keep others out. Spouses are first on this list because they are the closest to us. In relation to Christ forgiving our sins and taking us for who we are, our spouses do the same; at least they should. They love us no matter what. We seem to have a great deal of difficulty with this level of radical acceptance. People may also choose misery because it was the example they were given growing up. Being married means you are miserable. We joke about this, but in every joke there is a level of truth trying to be expressed.

> Psalm 107:10-12 says, "There were those who dwelt in darkness and in the shadow of death, prisoners in misery and chains, because they had rebelled against the words of God, and spurned the counsel of the Most High. Therefore He humbled their heart with labor; they stumbled and there was none to help."

David is speaking of those who chose to dwell in darkness and were "prisoners in misery." When we choose to abstain from practicing the fruit of the spirit, or when we choose not to make wise, spiritual decisions about our daily life, chains of the world will entangle us in the form of greed, depression, jealousy, etc. leaving us with unfulfilled lives. We do not do what God has instructed us for a fulfilling life; therefore, our lives are unfulfilling.

When there's not something deeper at play such as an addiction or infidelity, all many couples may need to do is choose. Will it be misery or will it be peace?

When you choose to notice everything your spouse does wrong, you are choosing misery. If you live with someone long enough, you are going to find plenty wrong. This is often a distraction in order to avoid your own shortcomings, but there you are, noticing all the inconsistencies of your spouse and wondering why you ever got married. Could you not have done better? He/she chews their food wrong or they breathe loudly through the nose. If you search for bad, you will find it. When you choose to argue rather than love, you are choosing misery.

There's something about being at war with your spouse. Some seem to enjoy it. We are not happy, and he/she is supposed to make us happy. *I'm not happy, so it must be your fault.* You are probably not happy because you are finding all of your spouse's faults and not working on your own. If you are one half of a whole that is supposed to be about love, what are you bringing to the table?

You choose misery when you think only of yourself. What can please me? This will lead to a most unfulfilling life. "When they are diminished and bowed down through oppression, misery and sorrow, He pours contempt upon princes and makes them wander in a pathless waste" (Psalm 107:39-40). Being in a relationship with another human being can be so rewarding. However, if you don't think of that other person, there will be no joy.

In his book, *Fall In Love Stay In Love*, Willard F. Harley, Jr. discusses needs and how important in a marriage is meeting the needs of your spouse. Much of the arguing in a marriage comes from not meeting one another's needs. It is strange, however, because this is really why we married in the first place; that person was personally fulfilling for us.

In reading the book, I discovered what my needs were. Strange that it happened this way, but not realizing my need for conversation caused a great deal of frustration in my life. However, when my wife and I realized what our top needs were, we could meet them. So, instead of engaging negatively, we work to be there for one another. Are you refusing to talk to her? Have you decided not to like what he enjoys? There will be war.

You choose peace, not misery, when you decide (or re-decide) to make a life with that person. Psalm 107:13-16 says,

> "Then they cried out to the Lord in their trouble; He saved them out of their distresses. He brought them out of darkness and the shadow of death and broke their bands apart. Let them give thanks to the Lord for His loving kindness, and for His wonders to the sons of men! For He has shattered gates of bronze and cut bars of iron asunder."

You choose peace when you offer forgiveness and a total acceptance of that other person despite his/her faults. You choose peace when you find some way to enjoy the time of being together rather than despising it. When you choose peace, you choose your words carefully, your actions carefully, and your thoughts carefully in order to make a life that you will enjoy seeing through your children once they begin their own life with another.

Marriage Purpose

Without a view of what your family should look like, it will turn into whatever your behavior leads you to. If your behavior is dictated by selfishness and the rat race of daily life, your marriage will suffer.

When a couple marries, they begin their journey as a couple. This journey consists of the "for better or worse" they vowed to endure. This journey gives both parties a sense of meaning and purposefulness. This married environment or purpose is not often discussed because couples are typically just thrown into it. It comes naturally through work, kids, friends, or church. All these give you something to do together which sort of oversimplifies what is actually happening.

For spouses that find satisfactory lives in solitude or who establish themselves without the other in mind, they lack marital purpose. Spouses need to feel that life without the other would be unbearable. Work would have less meaning, the kids would be less enjoyable, and your weekends would have less to look forward to if you were not with that other person.

Your work should bring you together as you discuss the day's struggles and triumphs. Although your spouse may be unable to handle the technical aspects of your job, he or she can give you a fresh perspective on the social and personal dynamics. Whom are you not getting along with? How can this change? Is your job affecting your marriage negatively?

Your work can also serve a marital purpose as it relates to your current financial status and future plans. Are you helping one another succeed? Do you support your spouse in advancing? This fills a need for the both of you on many levels. There is a financial reason and a level of fulfillment from winning that both of you can get from this. You are proud of the other as he or she succeeds.

Much of your energy is tied up in raising children. However, when they leave for college or to go on their own, it is just you and your spouse. You must be able to live with your spouse when the grand purpose of raising children is mostly over. So your current financial status must reflect your goals for the future. Work to make retirement happen. Work with a plan in mind now to be happy in the future. Finances are a big part of this plan. You can live off love, but you will starve.

Your children should bring you together as you work to raise them. We have children to form a powerful bond, enabling us to express a level of love that cannot be done in any other way. Not until my son was born did I fully realize the love God has for me. Raising children has truly helped me grow closer to my heavenly Father. Also, forming a new life is the grandest thing a couple can do together.

Your purpose can be about your children. Are you working to raise faithful Christians, people with strong character, people who will go further than you have in life, or all three? You work together as parents and purposefully to oversimplify this plan; you have something to talk about at the end of the day. You discuss where you think the kids are going, where you want them to be and how you can get them there. You share the responsibility, but also bring your own brand of personality to the parenting experience.

You do not want your purpose to be one of arguing. This is easy because couples tend to argue really well. They are bothered by their hard days at work and lash out at the people they see at home. They are dissatisfied with their marriage so they make each other miserable. They do not know what to ask for, and they do not know how to change it. This can be the culture that you have developed, and if it works, you will maintain it. It may be dysfunctional, but when you do not know how to do anything else, arguing and a stressful home life are then your culture.

Your purpose can be whatever you are both passionate about. However, the Word of God should be the hub of this. Whether your family is involved in scouting, martial arts, sports, or school activities, your Christian life should shine in all of these. The love of Christ and the example set forth in Scripture is the only true purpose that will make your home a happy one.

Christian Structure of the Home

Imagine losing your child to an accident. Imagine losing your child to an illness or any other unthinkable occurrences. Now imagine that your child had to die to save a world of ungrateful people, because it was the right thing to do for the state of the world. God's love for us is immeasurable. And what does He use to illustrate His relationship with us? The home, the marriage relationship, and the father/child relationship are all used to help us understand His depth of feeling. How should our Christian homes look?

One of the most controversial verses in Scripture is Ephesians 5:22-24.

> "Wives, *be subject* to your own husbands, as to the Lord. For the husband is the head of the wife, as Christ also is the head of the church, He Himself *being* the Savior of the body. But as the church is subject to Christ, so also the wives *ought to be* to their husbands in everything."

It is controversial because it is misunderstood. (I hesitate to generalize, but I think this is a safe place.) All institutions have some sort of leader; a head person responsible for the undertakings of those he or she is leading. Why should the institution of the home be any different? People are resistant to this idea because what Paul wrote to the Ephesians has been terribly mis-used. It has been used to justify a man's actions ranging from addiction even to spousal abuse. Misapplication is not what God intended.

In his book *Why They Left*, Flavil Yeakley does a masterful job of dissect-ing this verse for a world where women have more freedom than ever before. Yeakley first discusses the role of men in this passage. They are to love their wives as Christ loved the church. In doing this, a man should put his wife's needs before his own. This is known as servant leadership which is what Christ taught when He washed the disciples' feet. Men have a natural incli-nation to take care of their wives. Most of the time women do not see this as a man shows it through indirect means such as providing for the home.

Nowhere in Scripture is there a place that teaches women are inferior in any way. Yeakley says,

"Husbands and wives should seek to outdo each other in giving love, showing affection and giving service. Each should do what is best for the other. I believe that in the home as God would have it to be, most deci-sions are made by consensus. The husband and wife discuss things until they come to an agreement on what they will do. But there will be times when each wants to do what is best for the other, and they cannot agree. That, I believe, is when the husband as the spiritual leader of the family breaks the tie by deciding to do what is best for the wife."

If it turns out that he made a bad decision, he will learn from it. If it turns out that he made a good decision, the wife's confidence in his leadership will be strengthened.

A man who is a good leader will know his shortcomings and default to his wife when he needs her expertise. He will not buy a Mustang convertible when they have no savings. He will not start three hobbies in six months without mastering any of them. He will not let her have the grocery money when she does the grocery shopping.

First Corinthians 11:3 says, "But I want you to understand that Christ is the head of every man, and the man is the head of a woman, and God is the head of Christ." Inherent in the man leading his household is that he be like Christ. He most certainly has less say in things if he does not lead in a Christ-centered way. The woman must speak up. She must lead with her "chaste behavior" (1 Peter 3:2) and do what is best for her family's spiritual condition. When necessary, a wife should discuss why she disagrees with her husband, and she should strive to be like Sarah as Peter discusses her in 1 Peter 3:1-7. "In the same way, you wives, be submissive to your own husbands so that even if any *of them* are disobedient to the word, they may be won without a word by the behavior of their wives, as they observe your chaste and respectful behavior." Her leadership must be by example, but it must be vocal too when necessary as she does something that "is precious in the sight of God"—leading her family to Christ in the way God intended. As Jack Nicholson told Helen Hunt in *As Good As It Gets*, "You make me want to be a better man."

Some have dismissed Paul's teachings in 1 Timothy 2:13-14, a parallel passage, citing that his words were meant for only the people of the day. However, these instructions are based on the order of events in creation, not the culture of the first century. "For it was Adam who was first created, *and* then Eve" (verse 13).

Conclusion

Does your home look like God's model? Is it a place that your children will learn how to be good husbands? Good men? Good women? Good wives?

What do you want your child's home to look like when you visit on your grandchild's birthday? Do you want her to have an overbearing husband? Do you want him to be abusive or spineless? How do you want their home to look? You need to make your home look like that now.

How can a boy learn to be a man, and how can a girl learn to be a wife if these behaviors are not modeled. Does your own life reflect Titus 2:1-6? If not, neither will your children's.

Questions for Discussion

1. What elements of marriage are your children seeing on a regular basis? From you? School? Church?

2. What elements of a Christian marriage are important to show your children?

3. What system is at work in your home that follows the teachings of Ephesians 5:22-24?

PART 2 - MENTOR

CHAPTER 4

The Mentor—
Being Your Child's Teacher and Friend?

Parents envy the relationship their children have with their friends. The ease of discussion and the do-nothing time spent that seems so important are what parents long for. Being a child's friend is a terrible form of parenting. However, many attempt to raise their offspring with this method. It gives little direction and can serve only to validate an already misguided child. However, there are elements of friendship that some parent/child relationships can benefit from. I call it being a Mentor; a small, constructive role a parent can assume and that asks, "What can I teach my child?" This still means speaking with authority, but the dynamic that I have learned from my mentors is one that can work to bring a parent and child closer together. What can be bad about this?

Through this chapter and the next two, I want parents to lose the feeling that they are constantly reprimanding their child. Part of raising children is knowing how to mold them over time through positive interactions and a deeper understanding of their needs. A mentor understands this. By forcing them to follow you rather than leading them, you can cause them to be bitter toward you because the experience of being with you is so difficult to bear. Proverbs 9:8-9 says, "Do not reprove a scoffer, or he will hate you, reprove a wise man and he will love you." Your children are not terribly wise and they scoff at you a lot. The point of a mentor is to get your child to listen to you because you are such a great teacher.

Think of the mentors in your life, men or women who positively affected you and without whom you would not be the person you are today. Dr. Bill Greenwalt was one such man. We met once per week for supervision. These hours were going toward my licensure as a Professional Counselor. He would encourage my good ideas and chuckle at those he knew would not work. He was patient and always thought deeply about everything I said. These two virtues (patience and thoughtfulness) are hard to find. Dr. Bill Greenwalt died suddenly of a heart attack in January of 2006. I grieved deeply at his loss.

In the short memoir, *Tuesdays with Morrie*, Mitch Albom spends time with Morrie Schwartz, a former professor in the final months of his battle with ALS (Lou Gehrig's Disease). Morrie addresses what is really important in life and says that if people lived like they were going to die, they would live differently. They would live better. This is a prime example of one person sharing lessons he is learning/has learned with someone who is open and needs the life-altering wisdom.

Mitch was able to learn lessons from a man he admired at a pivotal time in both their lives. It has been said that when the student is ready, the teacher appears. I have been blessed with such relationships and for these I am eternally grateful.

No other debilitating sickness is quite like ALS. The body deteriorates, but the mind stays sharp. Another former mentor of mine was Don Chaffin. A minister at the Zion Church of Christ in Jackson, TN for many years, I realized very quickly one Sunday how many other lives he had touched. The building was packed on one of his last Sundays to preach. In a wheelchair and on his respirator, Don gave a stirring sermon from the Word of God. He did not tell us why we were destined for hell. He did not beat us up with a condescending attitude. Instead, he spoke with the love of Christ, and we listened. It was a man who was at the end of his life, and we wanted to know more because Don's attitude was one of grace.

Mentors are also a good source of guidance because they are seen as an authority. Parents are often tuned out when they say, "I was there once and here is what I did." And we say it so condescendingly. We do not offer it as a nugget of wisdom, but rather like we are forcing our child to believe like us. Did you struggle? Make sure your child knows you did. Were you scared? Talk about what that was like. Do not act like you are the final authority on the matter, but rather show you are better because of the experience and you want your child to know this. Help them see you as the mentor. Do not make them.

So that we do not have to plow through every mistake in life, the Lord blesses us with people who can light our way enabling us to realize our potential. The person may be a teacher who always knows your name or a supervisor who takes time for you no matter how busy he is. We need more people like this.

A mentor sees how the child can learn and embraces learning experiences. A parent may be quick to steer a child clear from things that could hurt the child. A mentor talks to the child. A parent can sometimes speak at the child. A mentor fosters a relationship where he can have a highly influential relationship. "Mom, can I stay up all night." You have told him a hundred times that he cannot, and you have told him why. This time you let him and allow him to pay the price the next morning. A good parent would have made him go to bed, but would continue to fight that nightly battle. A mentor knows how to teach a child with experience.

If you could teach your child something, what would it be? What lesson do you want to impart to your child more than anything? Are you living your life to teach this lesson?

The Mentor Mentality

As parents, we can sometimes be quick to judge, blame, and *force* our children to be shaped by our principles and values. We know where we want them to go in their growth. We see the end result, but are we starting in an appropriate place? Do we really see the child in front of us or do we see the child we wish we had? In the context of our lives, are we making the child we will be proud of?

Jesus taught people the greatest lessons known to man. He worked to reach people who did not know Him, who hated Him, and who wished Him dead. He really had to get His message out in an effective way. Parents must do the same because sometimes we are misunderstood and even hated for the actions we take with our children. Through the actions of Jesus, I think we can begin a new parent-child dynamic that opens the hearts of our children to what we want them to learn.

A mentor trusts that the lessons will be learned. A frustrated adult, at the end of a very short rope, will fail to see the value in working with his/her child. You have said it a hundred times, and you do not want to say it again. This is the job you signed up to do. By losing patience, you serve only to alienate the child from your wisdom as you express an unwillingness to see to it that the lesson is grasped. Your child will cut you off in the hopes that you will just quit bothering. Do not let this happen.

Why Teens Need Mentors

Teens have listened primarily to you for twelve years and now they want to know if it works. They see this is a job of separating from their parents. They strive for independence, and like a horse in the field, you must let them stray from your halter's grasp. Although teens need and crave this freedom, they actually need you more. They need you to let them roam, but they need you when they return. When a parent says, "What do you want now? Money?" he/she is setting up a dynamic with the child that expects only the worst. If you can show that you can meet your child's needs, he will be more readily available to approach you.

Teens need you more than they did even when they were children. They go out and come back. A child is there with you all the time, but for a teen to mature adequately, he must test your training. Plus, if your values and way of life are so good, they should work.

A mentor knows that children need to experience things to grow. You can watch a video on how to ski. I can teach you some survival skills for being in the backcountry. You can study a driver-training manual all week long, but until you actually take part in the experience, you are going to be missing something.

When you think of the mentors your child has, maybe a coach, teacher, or minister, they are all pretty patient with your child. These are, of course, those mentors your child likes to be around. This is a trait parents could really use with their children. Why is the mentor so good at it? Unlike a parent, they are not with the child as much. They see the child in their regular setting and that is it. No melt-downs in restaurants or in stores for a candy bar. Mentors do not have to argue over children's clothes or put them to bed. The child has lived with you longer and knows your weaknesses. A mentor also has less of a personal investment in the child. Doing well on the basketball court Saturday is not the same as doing well in life. Patience and the teaching of a skill are on their side. Plus, they can make a team member run as a consequence for a mistake. This gain in patience helps them to become less frustrated and more apt to teach.

Jesus as a Mentor

If Jesus was anything to His apostles, He was a mentor. He lived as an equal and showed them things through His actions. This is a difficult concept that was deeply covered in the model section. It is difficult because self-control and discipline are very difficult. A parent can cause trouble here by sacrificing good child-rearing principles for being less than what you would have yourself and subsequently your child be. To be clear, a parent is not equal with a child. There are things you get to do just because you are an adult. However, if you want to mentor the child, you must be who you say you want him/her to be.

If you are preaching to your child about eating right, you had better be eating right. I like to sneak a little late night snack once in a while. When I do this, I had better be prepared to give my son something too. He has the eyes of a hawk and the nose of a bloodhound when it comes to food. He knows. "Because I'm the parent" does not work in such times. You are the parent so you get to be fat? That is not a good line of reasoning, and it will hurt the relationship with your child. Jesus was the example to His disciples and when you become such to your child, you will find he/she has less ammo to use on you.

In Matthew 20:20-28 the mother of James and John asks Jesus if her sons can sit on His right and on His left. Jesus could have been very annoyed with them; trying to gain power over their peers, but He taught them a very important lesson. He did not try to shame them into humility but rather spoke to them of humility.

> "It is not this way among you, but whoever wishes to become great among you shall be your servant, and whoever wishes to be first among you shall be your slave; just as the Son of Man did not come to be served, but to serve, and to give His life a ransom for many" (Matthew 20: 26-28).

He understood where they were mentally and therefore was able to lead them where He needed them.

Not long after Judas makes his deal with the chief priests, he is dining with Jesus who calls him on his betrayal. Matthew 26:25 says, "And Judas, who was betraying Him, said, "'Surely it is not I, Rabbi?' Jesus said to him, "'You have said it yourself.'" I am sure that the tension grew in the room; no doubt a great deal of discomfort. Jesus had invested so much time with these men, and one actually finds a way to benefit himself financially. The synoptic Gospels give a similar account of Judas' betrayal. He speaks to the chief priests, Jesus makes the act known, and we do not hear from Judas again until they are all in the garden. On the other hand, John paints a bit more detail into this picture. John 13:30 says, "So after receiving the morsel he (Judas) went out immediately; and it was night." Jesus goes on to tell about

His pending departure from this world. The next time we hear of Judas is when he is bringing the Roman cohort to arrest Jesus.

Judas did not laugh at Jesus' comment, Thomas did not throw more doubt onto the matter, and Matthew did not change the subject. Judas was shocked at this reprimand and left to finish his plan because he was caught.

After Jesus' interactions with Judas, he goes on to tell the disciples, in Matthew 26:31 "'You will all fall away because of Me this night, for it is written, 'I will strike down the shepherd, and the sheep of the flock shall be scattered.'"" Then, Peter with the same confidence he no doubt displayed on the water when he stepped out of the boat says, "*Even* though all may fall away because of You, I will never fall away. Jesus said to him, 'Truly I say to you that this *very* night, before a rooster crows, you will deny Me three times.' Peter said to Him, 'Even if I have to die with You, I will not deny You.' All the disciples said the same thing too" (verses 33-35).

Be the Mentor Your Child Needs

As the mentor to these men, Jesus faced many things that parents face with their children. Jesus had to deal with their lack of faith that He possessed authority when they were on the sea and Jesus was asleep in the boat. Jesus had to deal with selfishness with James and John. Jesus had to deal with the frustrating task of teaching men that should know better. We use that last phrase with our children a lot. "You should know better," we tell our children. Because we cannot expect our children to be perfect, we need to let go of that frustration. Let go of what you want your child to be and grasp the concept that you are to help your child get to where you want them to be. On the hiking trail, I cannot wish that I was at my destination, I have to enjoy where I am. Be in the moment when you parent. Realize that your child does not know most things, will forget what you tell him, and will challenge you on most things. Your job is to balance that in order to head them in the appropriate direction. Getting angry will not help. What did Jesus do as the mentor to these men?

He listened. He did not cut them short when they had a concern. Jesus, being God on this earth, could know what they were thinking, but He always asked. He always let the people request what they wanted. He wanted their desire to come out of their mouth and heart, which enabled Him to connect. Think you already know what your child's question is, do not cut them off. Many children have a knack for asking again and again. This is simply a tactic to wear you down and to get what they want. Certainly, you must stop this behavior or it will drive you mad, but make sure you listen to your child.

Jesus led His people, which is what a mentor does. This may be splitting hairs, but help your child learn by leading them to the answer. Do not teach them as though they are a student at a desk. This conjures the image of lecturing which can be the most ineffective form of teaching. This is particularly true with teens. They want to figure things out. If you can help them do this, the lessons learned will stick longer. Lecturing and thinking you know what your child will say only serve to help them shut you out. They want to experience life. They want to trudge through the difficult moments. When you help them do this, you join with them and they learn. Parents are often quick to rush in and fix things to keep their children from having to bear an uncomfortable event such as a bad grade or a friendship issue. If you make this a habit of "fixing" things for your child, you will not help him/her develop self-reliance, but a dependence on you.

Jesus did not pass a final judgment on someone. He knew His Father would be doing this someday. He listened, stated what was right, and allowed the truth to come to the forefront. People had a hard time believing Jesus. Your children will have a hard time believing you. Do not resort to name-calling or yelling to get your point across to them. Jesus also understood the naivete of people. He knew that what he was saying challenged conventional wisdom and, therefore, would not be accepted by all. Your child is hearing stuff from television, school, and friends. They want to know what is right and have a hard time deciding on this. Your job as the mentor is to teach and, as we will see later, your job as the guide is to keep them safe.

You Can't Do Everything

Although the mentor mentality can go a long way in your relationship with your child, some things a parent cannot do. Of course, you do all the really important stuff, but some things that are just better left to other adults. Some would find it difficult to home school their kids by filling a teacher's role. I cannot teach my boy karate; I take him to class. Because you cannot teach your kid cooperation through team sports, you sign him up for football. Much of this is necessary in today's world because most people are no longer on the farm with several children. Much was learned in the earlier days due to tending gardens and livestock, and learning to get along with five or so brothers and sisters. Now we live in an age where we outsource our children to help them have a well-rounded experience in life. Do not be confused. As the parent you are still the primary influencer, but through extracurricular activities, your child can learn a great deal.

In 1 Samuel 1:11, Hannah, being distressed over not having a child, prayed, "O Lord of hosts, if You will indeed look on the affliction of Your maidservant and remember me, and not forget Your maidservant, but will give Your maidservant a son, then I will give him to the Lord all the days of his life, and a razor shall never come on his head." All of us want to give our children to God. We pray that they will be blessed servants of God. Hannah, later in chapter 1 takes Samuel to Eli to live in the house of the Lord.

This is truly a great sacrifice of a parent to give her child to another, but she was thankful for her blessing and knew that Eli would turn Samuel into a great man. In verses three and nine of chapter two, she makes a grand proclamation that all parents should heed when trying to raise their children in godly homes through the influence of other Christ-minded people. "Boast no more so very proudly, do not let arrogance come out of your mouth; for the Lord is a God of knowledge, and with Him actions are weighed." Then in verse 9, "[God] keeps the feet of His godly ones, but the wicked ones are silenced in darkness; For not by might shall a man prevail."

We cannot raise our children by ourselves. We cannot raise them effectively away from God, and we cannot raise them by the force of our hand. We must raise them in a loving, God-fearing home and know that others can help bear the burden of parenting as we look for those who can enrich our children's lives.

Interaction Cycles

What are your interactions like with your children? Productive or destructive? Positive or negative? Some parents may say that their time is always productive. This may be because they avoid difficult subjects like sex, friends, and drugs. Of course your relationship is nice; you never talk about the really important things your child may sincerely be struggling to overcome. Plus, chances are, that he will not bring it up. He will not know how to approach you, so you must study and determine when you should bring up things with your child. Make this a priority because your job as a mentor is to teach, and sometimes you must teach what your child really does not want to discuss because it is gross or uncomfortable. Get yourself over this fear, and open up communication today. It is not really about having "the talk" or having a talk about certain topics, but rather it is about having an open line of communication from the very beginning.

The times you spend with your child will not always be pleasant, but even in the most difficult of circumstances, they can be productive. If you have never had a deep conversation with your now thirteen-year-old, do not expect to have one this very evening, but you can grow into such talks. More about this in the next chapter. For the younger parents out there, have regular times during the day that you speak to your child. For my family, it is at bedtime. My son thinks about things (usually Legos or video games), and we discuss them. My hope is that when he is a teen, he will be comfortable enough to talk to me about other things. In any case, do not avoid talking to your child because you think it will be unpleasant. It is more unpleasant to clean up a mess and have to ask, "Why did we not talk about this sooner?"

With whatever you discuss with your child, you should strive to have what is called a Positive Interaction Cycle. This is where both parties feel heard and validated for their position and are seeking a deeper level of understanding. The opposite is a Negative Interaction Cycle which begins once someone starts yelling or has folded his arms and is on the defense. If you are not getting anywhere in your discussion aboard the angry train, you must stop, because your child will maintain this path. Remember, getting you angry is one method he/she can control. Jesus heard and listened to people; you must do the same. Do not be affected by the exact behavior of your child, but ask, "Why is he acting this way? Has someone hurt him? Is he confused?" These questions can help you discover the source of negativity in your family.

Of course, interaction cycles can be about the mundane. "What's for dinner, Mom?" to which you may say, "Why do you always ask that? I don't know." What should be a simple dialogue is now a negative interaction that will cause your son to speak to you less.

Do you have more positive or more negative interaction cycles? When his behavior is rude and you reprimand him, this is a negative interaction cycle (NIC), as it does not leave either party with a good feeling. These must happen, of course, but for some families, their entire system is based on this type of occurrence. The parents do not have the control they should or the child is consistently resistant to their corrections. Therefore, they are constantly redirecting his behavior. The key here is to limit the time these NIC's affect your relationship and work to capitalize on the positive interactions. Make them happen. When you must discipline your child, let this be the end of it.

Move away from the bad feelings you have and toward why you did what you did; you want your child to learn a different behavior. It is for his good and ultimately for everyone else's too.

Conclusion

When acting like a parent, we can alienate our children. We, their greatest teachers with the most personal interest in them, can push them away with our actions because we do not want them hurt, we do not listen; and we take our frustrations of parenting and anything else out on them. The mentor sees the value in experiencing life with his children and therefore uses all moments to teach and be with his children. Remember, this is what you signed up for.

Questions for Discussion

1. In what moments can you act as a mentor to your child?
2. What mentor attributes did Jesus exhibit the most?
3. How can you change negative interaction cycles into positive ones?

CHAPTER 5

Mentoring Your Child Through Difficult Emotions

The emotions of a child or teenager are a large point of contention in families. If these natural states can be better understood, home life can be much easier to handle. Emotions are natural responses to outside stimuli. Sometimes they go overboard and sometimes they are inaccurate. This is what maddens parents. "Why do you feel that way?" or "You're crazy" are just two of the responses beleaguered teens hear from the one they are to be learning from. Parents become so frustrated that they forget they are working with humans who are learning to harness and understand themselves.

If parents can become less engaged emotionally in a child's own struggle and then ask, "How can I help my child?" a parent can do his/her job better and the child will grow as a result. Life lessons must be learned and a mentor can help a child do just that.

Even the most well-intentioned parents can actually hinder their child's growth. As a mentor, you must be about the business of raising a child. As I have stated before, a mentor works to teach a child one thing. Well, you are charged with the task of teaching your child many things but actually just one—life. You do not want to keep a child, but you must work to help him grow into an adult.

"I Just Don't Understand Him"

Your Relationship

One of the reasons children and teens revert to their friends is that they are validated by them. But you and I know that this is nothing more than the blind leading the blind. Sure, your child can have some pretty bright friends, and maybe she is one of them. A brain-dead friend will have no idea what to do and may even give bad advice. When it comes down to it, you the parent (as a mentor) are what is best for her.

Some parents work to be their child's friend because they speak with such ease. However, when you speak to your child on this level, you lose the authority you should have as an adult. In my role as counselor, I am not a child's authority like a teacher, but neither am I at the level of a buddy where I tease or get teased by them. However, they speak to me in a way that they are comfortable because I am more like the mentor who leads them. You can do this too.

Where Are You Coming From?

When I work with parents of teens, they admit that they just do not understand their child. Well, there is an easy answer for this. Parents have lost their frame of reference regarding teen life. A frame of reference is what you draw from when working to understand just about anything. Movies utilize this concept well.

When you watch a movie, your frame of reference dictates whether or not you will enjoy it. If it is to be a big box office hit, there must be a central theme that everyone can comprehend. Most people, even non-comic book fans enjoyed the X-Men franchise because at its core, the series is about accepting people who are different. My wife enjoyed *Lord of the Rings*, because it is a love story between Aragorn, played by Viggo Mortensen and Arwen (Liv Tyler's character). This is a reference point most all women understand, and it ensures that they will not fall asleep or ask their husbands to leave the theater early. Amongst all the medieval rhetoric and mass killings of Orcs, a woman can empathize with Arwen as she works to win her man's heart; a thread Peter Jackson geniously wove throughout the twelve-hour movie.

In my middle school where I am a counselor, it is interesting to watch the 8th graders interact with the 5th graders when they come for a tour in the spring. "Oh, Look! How cute. They are so little." These same patronizing teenagers looked exactly the same way just three years prior. They have already forgotten how much they hated being called "cute" and how much they despised being canonized for their small stature. These adult-sized teenagers are much like parents who look down on their children for having irrational thoughts that always seem to ruin dinner.

In connection with Jesus' frame of reference, Hebrews 4:14 – 16 says this:

"Therefore, since we have a great high priest who has passed through the heavens, Jesus the Son of God, let us hold fast our confession. For we do not have a high priest who cannot sympathize with our weaknesses, but One who has been tempted in all things as *we are, yet* without sin. Therefore let us draw near with confidence to the throne of grace, so that we may receive mercy and find grace to help in time of need."

How much credibility would we give Jesus if this passage did not exist? This passage states that His experience brought us closer to Him. He knows what we go through and therefore we know that He can relate. We want to be like Him because this brings us closer to Him. Does this work with your children? Do they want to be the model you have set forth? Are you the mentor that brings them towards you so that they can get help?

Biology

Our brains change as we move from childhood to the teen years. We learn the best during our first eleven years. Scientists believe that when our brains change in middle school, it does so to make room for the capabilities of understanding abstract concepts; something we could not do at age five. Then, as we progress into our twenties, our brains mature, especially in males. I knew I was all grown up when I started listening to talk radio. No longer was I entirely self-absorbed, but I was interested in things that affected my family and the world around me. I had purchased a car, insurance, had a house, and a wife. I needed to think less of my score on Tony Hawk's Pro-Skater and more about the future I was now fully in control of. I was out of school and from that point on, everything I did, I chose. Had I been placed here at age fifteen or even eighteen, no amount of coaching would have enabled me for the endeavor. Like a good country ham, my brain needed to mature.

Another brain fact is that our memories are terrible. We are horrible at remembering things, and this is simple biology. The portion of our brain that stores memory is not the same that recalls it. So, there is a leap. You may remember that you did the exact same things your teen is doing, but chances are slim that you will remember exactly how you felt and even if you did, this is of little consequence to your teen. To him, the grunge age might as well be the Stone Age and remember, you want to understand *his* struggles now, not yours in the past.

Just Whom Are We Talking About?

Parents, you cannot understand your teen because you are not one, and using "when I was your age" as your only resource is unfair to you and to your kids. While humans have changed very little, the context in which humans are in has drastically changed. The leaps and bounds we have made in technology, and the various philosophies that have emerged as the result of our connected society, serve to enable today's child to experience and see things more than any other child in history. They are no longer confined to the small Mayberry-type communities, but, in seconds, can learn about pornography on their phone or speak to someone through video a world away.

To our favor, humans have actually changed very little. Think about if you were alive in the days of Sodom and Gomorrah. You or your grandfather would have said things like, "The world is changing. There won't be a heterosexual person left if they keep this up." If an insightful person were to have asked you before the fire and brimstone incident, "Where do you think our society will be in the 21st century?" your response would probably not be terribly positive. However, look where we are. There are still good people, fighting for what is right.

You can look at the world only through adult eyes. It is impossible for your teen to do this. He has not been an adult. You must imagine his world now. Understand his context and struggles, even conjure your own feelings about the same events, but not to show him you succeeded. Rather, so you can better help him. Then, you can work on some things that will help you do what you need to do for your child.

Understand Her Better

First, understand her world in her context. Realize that looking through the world with teen eyes can help you understand and then lead your child as a mentor should. The bantering I hear in my office and in the hallway is endless. Who your friends are is life and death in the mind of a child and teenager. This of course morphs over time. In elementary school, you are friends with whoever is nice. In middle school, you want to be friends with whoever everyone else wants to be friends with. In high school, you are a little more independent, but social stature is still crucial.

If she comes home crying because her three best friends in the whole world wore matching socks and did not include her, avoid the mistake of dismissing this traumatic event. She wants to fit in. She wants to be accepted. It is the greatest feeling in the world, and when she is ignored for two seconds at lunch, it is the end of the world. Validate her feelings. Acknowledge that she is hurt. While these things are unimportant to you, they are paramount to her. The "valley of the shadow of death" spoken of in Psalm 23 is in your child's school hallway. She will face difficulty, but you can help.

Second, help her work through it logically. We as parents know that the day of sock exclusion will later be forgotten. But just as we would not leave our child soaking in a mud-puddle, we should not leave her to figure out the simple complexities of the middle school social fabric. When she is less emotional and thinking a little more, help her understand what is happening. Did she forget she was supposed to wear them? Are the girls really excluding her? Why did they not tell her? Does she need new friends? Then, you can bestow your best heart-felt wisdom. While she may not see the value immediately, she is learning to sort the issue in her head in a way that makes sense. It does make sense to her that these girls left her out on purpose, and this hurts. However, it does not make sense that she should lose sleep over a group of girls who obviously are not good friends. You can get her to this place, and she will love you for it.

Third, do not work to make sense of something that does not make sense. We feel this way quite often after talking to our teens about the latest drama they have brought home. And why not? You are dealing with an amateur in a world of amateurs when it comes to living. Listen to him, but in the end, when you are both confused, trust your parenting. Do not allow him to do whatever it is he is confused about doing if you both do not know what to do.

Your Behavior Affects Theirs

A mother approached me once with some concerns about her son. She described him as being anxious; a worrier. After a brief discussion, I asked about his father. She said that his father/her husband was very active in their son's life, but went on to say that she believed her son's anxiety had a lot to do with his father. "My son," she said, "worries about what his dad thinks of his athletic ability. In fact," she continued, "a lot of the boys on his team are the same way with their fathers." Worried that he will not play his best on the field, her son becomes anxious. Mom believes this may carry into other areas of his life. I agree.

I have seen this behavior before both as a player and spectator. My hand on the ball in the middle of 1200 high school football fans, I could hear one particular woman screaming at us. I know this had a negative effect on her son. While watching middle school basketball, I have observed players glancing in the stands at their parents after each pass or shot as if to say, "How was that?" The child, consequently, is playing two opponents. One she is trying to outplay and the other, mom and dad, she is trying to please.

No doubt there are parents who push their children so much that emotional issues are inevitable. However, the mother I mentioned at the start made it clear that her husband was not one of these. He was a proud father who watched his son with enthusiasm, but did not relentlessly push him to perform. So, what is going on? Why does a father who is not overbearing cause his son anxiety on the field? Was the child naturally anxious? Maybe. Some personalities lean in this direction. Was dad doing something that he did not realize? Possibly. Anxiety can be produced in a child by some of the most well-equipped parents. Let's look at what may be happening.

Let's say Mason, the son, plays well and gets regular praise from his parents. This is good, but what happens when he does poorly? There is less excitement; nobody feels like post-game milkshakes, and the encouragement you try to offer probably is not welcomed. Especially if he thinks you are just trying to make him feel better, as every caring parent would want to do. These are all typical occurrences after a loss. What is also typical is what may be happening in Mason's mind as he filters the events that follow a poorly played game. After a win, everyone is happy. After a loss, everyone is sad. The coach (typically a male) is disappointed; the players are disappointed; and the ride home is quiet and depressing. With all these negative cues adding up in your son's head, the following belief could formulate. "If I please you when I do well, then I must be displeasing to you when I do poorly." It's likely you do not believe this, but certain messages after a loss can culminate in this belief. It is no one's fault really because these are natural responses to what is happening, but parents must work to counteract them.

So, what should you do? First, you can offer a listening ear after a loss. His own self-criticism might be difficult for you to bear, but because he is in an emotional state, logic and reason are not going to make it into his vocabulary. So don't offer it. He may say, "I hit like a two-year-old!" Just let him vent. Second, when he is less emotional, you can offer sincere encouragement by helping him see what he did well and validate what he needs to improve on; especially if he mentioned it. Maybe he did hit like a two-year-old, and could use a few hours in the batting cage. This will help him gain an appropriate perspective on his ability by seeing the good and the bad, which will lead him toward improvement. Finally, if you believe you are inadvertently causing anxiety in your child, what you do between games that can make the biggest difference.

When he does something well, it's natural and exciting to point this out. But do you ever tell him, for no particular reason, that you appreciate him? He knows you love him. It's what you're supposed to do, but do you ever let him know that you're glad he's your son? Grades, sports, or social status aren't referenced. You're just glad he eats dinner with you. Because this happens less naturally, a conscious effort must be made to let Junior know that he's tops in your book. Giving random gifts, praise for something that took work, but that might otherwise go unnoticed, and quality time over a sundae at Baskin Robbins for no reason at all can do wonders for your child's perception of what you think of him. Conveying your feelings will not trigger an unshakable self-confidence overnight, but little by little it will build within him the belief that he is worth something, not because of his athletic performance but because he is yours and with this self-concept, he will be able to conquer anything because you are on his side.

How Much Is Praise Worth?

Want to improve your child's self-esteem? Praise him constantly and thwart anything that may hurt his perception of being an intelligent person. With every success, your child will see that he is a winner and will continue to achieve. Sounds like good advice doesn't it? Well, it is terribly misguided.

In the spring 1999 issue of *American Educator*, Carol S. Dweck's article entitled, "Caution—Praise Can Be Dangerous" examines the effects of praising children.

In almost 30 years of research Dweck has found that children who were constantly praised could not adapt well to new challenges. They were obsessed with their intelligence and with proving it to others. These children constantly feared failure and believed that not succeeding at a task meant they were dumb. This stifled their growth leading them to give up easily or not to try at all when they perceived something was too difficult. Dweck also knew of students who did not pride themselves as much on their intelligence but rather their work ethic and ability to face challenges.

A study on the two groups was done to see if praising children for being intelligent could cause them to become dependent on praise. One group (Group A) was praised for their intelligence in working a puzzle, "Wow, you must be smart at this." and another group (Group B) was praised for their effort, "I can tell you worked really hard." The result? Group A wanted to quit when they were given a more difficult puzzle, but Group B enjoyed the new challenge and was willing to work harder.

In summary, Group A's confidence depended on their success with the problems. The group members needed praise believing that if they couldn't do something well, they would rather not do it at all. Group B simply saw the more difficult problem as a challenge and was willing to put forth the effort to solve it. Group A crumbled under the pressure, but Group B retained their intellectual self-esteem.

So, what should we do? Dweck recommends focusing on a student's potential to learn, teaching each to value challenge and learning over looking smart; and finally, teaching concentration on effort and learning. Otherwise, a lost ballgame or F on a test could weaken an already fragile self-image.

What if the outcome is not favorable, and your child still did his best? Encouragement is what is needed here and in almost every situation. There is a small, but definite, difference between this and praise. Tell your child that he is a hard worker or that you are proud of the way he handled a particular situation. This will let him know that you believe in him and don't place his self-worth on being perfect. Then, as tougher challenges arise, he will answer them because he believes in his own strengths and does not need the constant praise of others.

Conclusion

Our hearts break when our children are hurting. Our blood pressure rises when they come to us with things that do not make sense. We agonize over the fact that our offspring will not speak to us. By working to understand your perspective, and your child's, the gulf between the two of you can be drastically shortened. It is put there by the behavior you engage in, but by changing your behavior to the kind that fosters a positive parent/child relationship, you can be the mentor your child needs.

Questions for Discussion

1. How can you work to understand your child's perspective better?

2. What behaviors do parents exhibit that intensify their child's already intense behaviors?

3. Explain the difference between praise and encouragement.

CHAPTER 6

The Mentor's Gift
of Communication

Communication Among Parents and Kids

Think of the last time you spoke to your child. Was it pleasant? Was it like pulling teeth? Was he like my four-year-old son who seems to talk non-stop? An adult talking to a teen can be especially difficult. You are of another generation, and you don't understand how the phrase "Bad to the Bone" was replaced with the word "sweet." Having a decent conversation is a struggle, and you can forget about having a meaningful one. "The Talk" is a quick in and out. Your son closes the door to his room just as you finish, "How was your... (SLAM)... day?" "Fine," comes muffled through his door as he sits down to Instant Message his friends he just saw 30 minutes ago.

Opportunities to affect our children positively come by way of moments when we can verbalize our opinions and values to them. The dangerous thing is that adults often make the least of these opportunities and ruin an otherwise meaningful event. We as parents make mistakes because we're human, but also because we don't understand some basic tenets of talking to our children and teens. As parents look to mold their children, they should be careful of the words they choose, the body language they employ, and the tone in which they speak. Even though parents have the final say in matters dealing with their children, how they communicate this message is extremely important. When you ask them, "Are you listening?" you want them to be able to say, "Yes."

Parental Communication vs. Mentor Communication

As a youth minister, I would often go and say "hello" to the faculty and to the students during lunch at our local high school. As I was leaving, a visibly enraged mother was verbally scolding her son with intense enough speech to bolster the Nazi regime. We got in our cars at the same time, and I could still hear her screaming at him; arms flailing and head shaking.

One day in my office, a more than slightly disgusted father yelled at his fourteen-year-old daughter, ". . . and don't call me at work again to bail you out!!" The young lady's outfit did not meet dress code and dad had to leave work to bring her some new clothes. I'm sure she won't call again. I wonder though just what else she won't tell him.

When I was a teenager, I met a man by the name of Jeff Archey. He very quickly became my mentor as he took a genuine interest in me and my desire to become a minister. When he heard me preach, he would give constructive thoughts, and I would eagerly listen. The mentor is there to shape and to mold. Parents can do this too, but some must start doing things differently.

Adopt A No-Yelling Policy

I know what high school and middle school students are capable of, and I know that parents become very frustrated with their offspring. However, yelling will never change a child's behavior. A raised voice to get a child's attention or to communicate a parent's intensity is beneficial, but yelling to try to change something a child does will have little to no effect. It is the equivalent of fighting on the playground to end a conflict; you have run out of ideas.

Think about how you would want to be spoken to at your job or by your spouse. Imagine that these people you trust begin yelling at you for something you did wrong. "CAN'T YOU DO ANYTHING RIGHT? I'VE TOLD YOU 100 TIMES NOT TO DO THAT!!" I am sure that after this tongue lashing you are sure to never forget to take out the trash again. I am also sure that this sort of speech will cause you to become a better student, a better brother, and a better child in general. Of course not. These words only make you recoil like a snake, ready to strike.

In the child who withdraws because of the constant beating he receives verbally, his rebellion is slowly churning and bubbling, waiting to be unleashed. This may be when he leaves home, or it may be when he finally decides he's going to say something to the parent who has constantly berated him all this time. Then, the relationship is finally seen for what it is; a relationship built on harsh words, sarcasm, and the inability to speak positively with one another.

Parents can talk to their kids however they want. The question must be asked though, "Is what you are doing good for your child?" Ephesians 4:29

says, "Let no unwholesome word proceed from your mouth, but only such a word as is good for edification according to the need of the moment, so that it will give grace to those who hear." Say what you want, but will it bring about the desired result you want from your child?

Proverbs 25:11-12: "Like apples of gold in settings of silver, is a word spoken in right circumstances. Like an earring of gold and an ornament of fine gold is a wise reprover to a listening ear." You're human, you're going to lose your cool with your child, but don't you always want to be in your prime? Don't you want to be playing your A-game constantly? If so, this verse should have a great deal of meaning. When your child does something wrong, would not a well-placed word be much better than screams?

Proverbs 13:3: "The one who guards his mouth preserves his life; The one who opens wide his lips comes to ruin." Even as parents, we speak too quickly and too harshly sometimes. I have found that I raise my voice with my son mostly when I am tired. I am sitting down reading, writing or enjoying my freshly ground coffee, and I do not want to get up and fix his latest toy that just crashed to the floor. But you see, I am being lazy. He is just being a kid.

Raising one's voice to emphasize a point can be helpful. To show emotion and communicate one's seriousness is important. Get his attention with a little higher volume, but you do not have to be angry. Your child is learning and may or may not know what he has done. Also, yelling at an unsuspecting child causes a fight or flight response. It doesn't open him up to understanding. Instead, he becomes agitated and may begin yelling back.

You Must Understand Your Child's Thinking

I work with middle schoolers. This age group has its own unique challenges. They are sometimes immature enough to be considered children and sometimes mature enough to be called young adults, but they are full-time teenagers. Because of these attributes, they can be very challenging.

During the fall semester, I try to teach on at least one topic per month. This can be difficult since I am not in the class with them every day. So, to keep the students engaged in the learning process, I employ magic, group work, videos, and even a football-shaped party clapper. It's about 10 inches by 8 inches, and when you shake it back and forth, it makes a tremendous sound. This gets the students' attention and adds a bit of excitement to an otherwise boring time of discussion. I will sometimes even allow students to use it, especially if they aren't participating that much.

During an 8th grade lesson, one student asked me if he could use the clapper. He had acted inappropriately earlier so he was not on my good side. He asked me about three more times when I finally said, "No, and when you ask me again in five minutes, the answer will be the same." I thought to myself, "Oh no." It was like I was playing poker with him and had just showed him my cards. "Bet whatever you want, big guy. The money is yours." If you have a teenager you know what I said, and sure enough, SIX minutes later, he asked, "Mr. Sadler, it's been six minutes. Can I use the clapper now?" I said, "Sure" and handed him his trophy.

Some teenagers have this strange desire to beat us at our own game. Adults talk about how they are in charge and how what they say is law and how children should always listen to adults. Did he listen to me? Of course he did. Was his behavior maddening? Yes! Do middle schoolers just like to push our buttons sometimes? You bet, but had I sent him to the office, I would have lost. No amount of discipline would have proved him wrong; at least in his eyes. I said five minutes and he was only following what I had said.

In the world of adults we know that what he did was disrespectful, but when working with teens you sometimes have to play by their rules, which in this case were rules set up by adults. "Do what I say." I knew I messed up when I made the statement originally, so I did the only thing I could that would bridge the gap from me to him. Had I given him a much-deserved scolding, he wouldn't have liked me very much. He would have lost respect for me, and the chances of him doing what I asked in the future would be slim because I am obviously not a man of my word.

Three things to remember when speaking to teens:

1. They will hold you to your word, so be careful of what you say.
2. They don't like feeling as though they've been lied to, so watch what you promise.
3. They can't often make sense of what they are thinking, so be there to help them figure it out.

Although they are your children, you can address them in ways that are not conducive to a positive interaction. I am not saying you can never get angry with your children, but I am saying if you break some of the following guidelines, you'll have a tougher time reaching them.

First, they will hold you to your word, so don't say things you don't mean. I run CARE teams at my school. CARE stands for Children Are Resilient and

Empowered. Once per week for two to three months I meet with students ranging in groups of three to eight in number. During a particular session, one young lady talked of her frustration about how her dad was telling his step-daughter to move out if she wanted to. Apparently the two had been arguing over household rules, and the girl said how she wanted to move out. Dad began encouraging this. Once the smoke had cleared it was plain to see that no one really wanted anyone to move out. So, why say it? What purpose does it serve? Although it is every kid's dream to move out of his parents' house at age 13 and every parents' dream that they move out at age 12, neither party really means it. So, why say it? There may come a time when you will need to do this, but the first time you want to is not it.

In these heated arguments, the child, wanting to hurt a parent, may suggest such an outrageous notion. This is particularly typical in divorced homes where the child is arguing with her custodial parent, and in a fit of pubescent rage she says, "I want to live with Daddy." Has she thought about the changes this would bring or the difficulty in getting it done or the fact that living with someone every other weekend is much different than living with them all the time? No, of course not. The parent, frustrated, out of ideas, and not wanting to back down from her principles, suggests that it might not be a bad idea. "It only makes sense. You're fifteen and you know everything. Why shouldn't you move out?" This might seem like the logical conclusion based on your current emotional state, but it is not usually a plausible idea; especially if the child has nowhere to go.

As this option rears its head in difficult moments, the child begins to follow through with it. Not knowing where to turn, she has been told that she can go. So, she calls Grandma, Aunt, or her friend from math class and begins her new life while packing her bag. The child, being such, is only following through with what she's being told. Depending on adults to offer guidance, this is the logical step. However, it all comes crashing down, and confusion ensues when Mom or Dad says she cannot move out. The bluff of the parents has suddenly backfired.

Second, they don't like feeling as though they've been lied to, so watch what you promise. Kids today are lied to entirely too much. I speak to many in divorced situations who agonize over the fact that Mom or Dad did not visit them last weekend even though they promised. The last thing kids need is yet another adult not doing what he said he was going to do. To Mr. Six Minutes, I acknowledged what I said and followed through with its implied logic. He was a big help for the rest of the period clapping away for those with correct answers. I could teach him later about how his behavior was inappropriate. Teens already have a difficult time trusting anyone over 25. The noise in their heads is deafening. They need someone around to know what to do. They certainly don't. If you lie, you are not dependable, and why should the child honor or respect that? You must be about the business of doing exactly what you say.

Third, because they cannot often make sense of what they are thinking, be there to help them figure it out. Kids don't think like adults. Adults are given a scenario and are able to consider the potential outcomes. If teens could do this, they would not need adults. Once kids turn thirteen they act like they know everything, but all they really know is how to run their MySpace page. Not much else really matters to them. Dad gives me money. Food goes in here. What else is there for survival? If they were good at decision-making, they would wait for marriage to have sex, and they would quit using prime time television as their moral compass.

As I work with my middle schoolers, I hear a common theme. "My parents don't listen." It's strange because when I talk to parents they often say, "My teen won't talk to me." I find fault with parents and teens in these situations. Teens, believing that parents will only scold them, hold back information and form a general unwillingness to talk with Mom and Dad. Parents often give their teen a reason to believe this way. Making a teen feel shame for having sexual desires will only cause him to bear much unwarranted guilt and an unwillingness to go to Mom or Dad when the desires become too much. Then, instead of getting accurate information, he acts on his impulses and pays the price through a guilt-ridden conscience, the contraction of STD's, or an unwanted pregnancy.

A basic tenet of being a teenager is figuring things out. When a parent rushes in to fix everything, this causes the teen to withdraw from any help the parent might want to give. They need help figuring it out. They don't want someone just giving them the answer. Well, maybe in Geometry class, but certainly not in life. This brings us to a very important topic. As your child becomes a teenager, you must stop trying to show him things. You must teach him things in the truest sense of the phrase. I know this sounds like heresy, but let me explain.

As you bring up your child, you teach him to be polite. You teach him to play and to color. He knows little of what the world is so he makes sense of it as you teach him. A teenager on the other hand has heard it all before. "Don't chew with your mouth open." "Don't talk so loud." "Don't say those things." A teenager is trying to live in a world as a human being. Before, he was a clone of you, and now he is some sort of rogue ship going against your travel plan and heading right into open water. Because you taught him manners, built up character in him, and showed him what is important to your family, he wants to go into the storm to see if what you have taught him really works. By holding him back you may protect him in some ways, but you hinder his spirit from growing and being all that it can be much like the eagle raised with chickens who never learns to soar as he really can. When you say, "That doesn't make any sense" to something they are communicating, it probably doesn't make sense to them either. There must come a time when you enforce the "that's crazy" rule. Don't tell them this but what they are seeing is likely crazy. Help them wade through the pollution in their brain put there by their peers and MTV, and help them see what reality is.

Word Choice Is Important

I just finished listening to a lecture by Dr. James Garbarino, professor of human development at Cornell University. His presentation, "Parents Under Siege: Raising Children in a Socially Toxic Environment" was insightful as he discussed cultural influences on our children. It was also eye-opening because it helped me see that I had a bad habit in regard to a particular parenting skill. Through my studies, I consider my actions as a parent, husband, and human being. I would be a hoax if I didn't. Garbarino discussed how children do not view adults, including their parents, as authoritative. Teens undermine the power of adults and even question their right to be in charge in the first place. Garbarino went on to explain that it's a particular act of parents that may contribute to this character trait. He gave the following example that got my attention because I do it.

When parents speak to their children, they sometimes end sentences with the word, "OK." Let's go to bed, OK? Let's eat our dinner, OK? This two letter word turns what should be an unshakeable command into a question a request. This child, who should have little freedom besides what the parents give them, is being asked what he wants in almost every situation because of the word, "OK." Parents should ask some things of their children because they are an important part of the family. This democratic style of parenting keeps the doors open to regular communication. When he's 15, he will be more likely to reveal what is going on in his life because you've appropriately included him in family decision-making and discussions over the years.

Aside from this, children should have little input. They are not in charge, and would rarely make the decision that is best for all involved in the same way the parent would. When given a choice, my son will always choose Thomas the Train over sleep. So asking, "Let's go to bed, OK?" is ridiculous. As soon as I understood this concept my mind began to race through all the times I had done this. Let's get in the car, OK? Let's put your shoes on, OK? This warmed my heart because it encouraged communication between us as he would often respond verbally. In my defense, I always did what I intended to do no matter what he said. "Let's go home, OK?" I often asked. He would give an innocent "Nooooo" and then I would say, "Tough" as I playfully scooped him up. Nevertheless, if I continued this asking phraseology, he would grow up thinking that he had a say in everything we do.

Children are difficult enough to raise; they don't need to be given the idea that we need their approval. Cotton candy and TV until 3 am would be a nightly routine if some had their way. As you're ready to rush out the door and you tell your five-year-old to put on his socks and shoes, or get his bag, this may be too much for him. When directing a child, you must think as a child. Much of my son's anxiety while we're getting ready, comes from me. I wait too late to get him going and his speeds of slow and stop just can't catch up.

Be definitive and clear, not ambiguous and suggestive. "Clean your room" could mean a lot of things especially to a young child or to a teen who doesn't care what his room looks like. Kids are not born with a sixth sense of how to organize. They must be taught it. "Put your toys in the toy box" is much clearer. "Come home early" to you may mean 10 pm, but to your teen it may mean before the sun comes up. "Be home by 10 pm" is much more meaningful and clearly communicates what you want. If left open to interpretation, your daughter will take unspoken liberties, giving you a heart attack.

The Language of Choice

If we are going to reach children and teens, we must understand how they think. Otherwise, they won't let us teach or, for that matter, parent. One tactic that can give you strength beyond measure is the language of choice. Relinquish some of your need to control your child and give your child some control. You don't lose authority as a parent, but you allow your child to have an appropriate amount of control teaching them things through experience rather than lecture. The lesson my four-year-old son learns while wrecking his bike (with pads and helmet) is much better than an hour long exposition of the physics of falling as it relates to the mechanics of one's bike.

Kids and teens like two things that you can give them a great deal of—power and attention. The power can be given through the language of choice. A friend of mine, told me that his three year old was a real chore in getting him to go to bed. However, when he gave him a choice of what to go to bed with, there was no problem. You see, my friend gave his son a choice in what was appropriate. He asked his son, "Do you want to sleep with your dog or your monkey." Sleep was not an option, but what to go to bed with was because the choice could be given to him. In not wanting to go to sleep, the boy exercised the power he had not going to sleep. No parent can make a child go to sleep, but a parent can give his or her child options. The boy didn't want to avoid sleep, in fact, your child has probably acted the same way when he or she was extremely tired. The child is enacting power that they have. Give them power in areas they can have it.

This helps them develop confidence in that you trust them. It helps them develop reasoning ability and brings them out of a shell that they might develop with you as a parent doing everything for them all the time. When you give your child or teen choices, it allows them to employ what they've been taught over the years, which is a large stepping stone for them. Treating them as if they're younger than they are can cause hurt. "Don't you think I can do it?" "Don't you trust me?" The innate desire of our offspring is to get away from us. As badly as that might hurt some parents, all of them want to be on their own at some level. There's no prouder moment than when Mason does something on his own.

Lecturing takes a lot of energy; they won't remember it, and tearing them down to build them up only works in the military. They don't want to listen to us sometimes because they hope that we are brave enough and trusting enough to let them learn some things on their own. These are the greatest lessons.

The Saturday before I left for a week-long Bible camp at Fall Creek Falls State Park, my mother must have said a thousand times, "Don't put your wet towels in with your dirty clothes. They'll get mildewy." Mildewy? That sounds pretty cool. All week long I heard her words in my head, but it was raining all week so they weren't going to dry anyway. What could it hurt? My nose. That's what it hurt. The lesson, although only a hygienic one, was one I have never forgotten because I learned it on my own.

This language of choice allows them the freedom to make mistakes within reason and sets them up to choose consequences you have set forth for inappropriate behavior. This will be covered in another section. "You came home late so you have chosen to be grounded next weekend. You used the cell phone when I asked you not to so you have chosen not to have it for a week." It teaches them their behavior has consequences.

How to Listen

Until they truly mature, teens are living in such a way that is safe for them. Because keeping quiet and blending in with a group is safe, getting a teen to open up can be difficult. They play it safe by keeping quiet, but they will not grow unless they discuss things. This is one of the reasons they are on social networking sites like MySpace and Facebook. They are trying to discover their path in life in a safe environment. It has its dangers, but the internet can be safe because there is anonymity, and it can be turned off. You need to work at being a major influence here, but sometimes parents mess this up by not listening. God gave us two ears and one mouth. Even parents need to listen twice as much as they speak.

Teens say very little because sometimes they are afraid of what you will say. They want to tell you, but past experience may have taught them not to trust you. Let us say, for example, they came to you with something, but instead of listening, you went into a long exposition of what they should do. Remember, help them figure things out. This is impossible to do unless you listen.

First, you must avoid interruptions. Give her plenty of time to think. Adults often interrupt teens in less than five seconds. They need more time. If she is thinking, she will look around the room or bite her lip. If she is in a daze, she is just waiting for you to say something like you always do. Bring her back around and encourage her to talk by assuring her you will not interrupt until she is done.

When it is time for you to step in, she will begin to stumble over her words, take a breath and sigh, or say something like, "I am just not sure." It is here that you can tell her what you think. Do not be afraid to do this, but be sure to state why you think the way you do. If she argues, listen again. Maybe you do not understand totally. She very well could be wrong, but you definitely need to communicate why you are right if that is indeed the case.

However, if she does not think you are right, what good have you done?

Second, watch what you say when telling her what you think. If her boyfriend just dumped her, she does not need to hear that he was a no good bum. If he was, what does that say about her? She dates no good bums. You are not helping. If he was not worth her time, she will see that later, but a broken heart is no place to lay fault or blame. Any little thing that she hears will be heard through the filter of, "what is wrong with me." Speak with purpose in such a way that she will feel better. If you do not know what to say, say nothing. The right words will eventually come.

Conclusion

They are your kids and you need to tell them what you think. However, you want what you tell them to stick. Wanting to fix things right then and becoming emotional without any regard to how your words will affect your child are all mistakes parents make. A mentor on the other hand uses events to teach and chooses their words wisely. Anything else might result in your child (the student) not listening. Your influence will be reduced and the influence of others will creep into your child's life. Do not let this happen and work at communicating well with your child.

We have one chance to raise our children. It starts and ends with what we say to them.

Questions for Discussion

1. What common "parental" phrases can you eliminate for more docile "mentor" lines that are easier to hear and are more constructive?

2. In what circumstances is yelling appropriate and constructive?

3. Compare/contrast a child's thinking with that of an adult.

PART 3 - GUIDE

CHAPTER 7

The Guide—
The Role That Only You Can Fill

The final portion of my theory I call "The Guide." It has most of the characteristics people would equate with parenting and asks the question, "What must I ensure that my child learns?" I do a lot of hiking. Upon finishing this book, I plan on making it a bigger part of what my son and I do. Our children spend so much time in a classroom and in front of the television; we really must make a concerted effort to put things in their lives that will shape them. Experiences such as hiking, sports, and anything outdoors can do this. I am a proponent of sports in kids' lives, but even if you are the coach, you really are not doing the activity with your son. Hiking, archery, and fishing are different. It is you and your child, not you, your child and fifteen other kids. Hiking is a good metaphor for life and particularly parenting.

My hikes range anywhere from six miles to thirteen miles to overnight trips. Because the locations are so remote, I get to see things no one else can or ever will see because getting in (and getting out of) these locations is no easy task. I have always had a love for the outdoors. My parents and I would go camping and swimming in the creeks on my great uncle's property in Red Boiling Springs, TN. We would also go fishing regularly, and of course, church camps always bring us closer to nature.

I started hiking with my dad and a friend of ours when I was in high school. These experiences always seemed to bring us closer together because being deep in the woods exposes you in many ways. While at home, we have homework to do, jobs to worry about, meals to fix, and even calls and messages to answer. While on the trail, nothing is separating you from those you are with except your own consciousness. You can choose not to speak to those you are with, but it will be a long trek. On the other hand, you can open up and discuss important topics that will leave you with a level of clarity that an afternoon in front of the TV could never give you. Time moves quickly through our days while we try to connect with our children, but it creeps along on the trail and we are able to soak up every moment.

Although hiking is safe, it is also dangerous. You could simply twist an ankle and be stuck overnight, or if you are hiking in the northwest, your hierarchy on the food chain drops drastically. I have taken several friends with me on hikes, and they have loved every moment. Some have even gone on to be more obsessed than I about getting out into nature. So it goes with parenting. We travel along in life with our children in the hopes that they will not make the same mistakes we did, and that they will be better than we were as teens and go on to be more successful adults.

Imagine that you are an inexperienced outdoorsman about to go on his first hike. You have a few supplies and some decent shoes. You arrive at the trailhead, and your guide gets out of the truck with a 40-pound pack. Suddenly, the soda and Snickers bar you brought with you seem like they will not suffice. Your guide, recognizing your hesitancy, smiles and says, "Don't worry, I have enough for both of us." You are relieved. He has invited you because he enjoys nature and knows you will too. As you begin, he points out things you have never seen before. He shows you the wild growing ferns on the forest floor and even gives you a sassafras leaf stem to chew on.

Your hike continues. There's no cell phone service; you pass other hikers who have twice the gear you do, and your feet begin to get wet after misinterpreting the depth of a puddle. You plod on because your guide is confident, and other things make the hike enjoyable such as the conversation. You stop to look at a millipede and the mountain laurel that seems to go on forever. Light barely seeps in through the trees and you have never been here before, but despite your reservation, you continue because you trust your guide.

After a couple of hours, you sit to rest. Your brain processes the length of your trip thus far. It seems you have been gone for days. Your legs ache, and your back is tired. The banana you pull out of your bag is *the* best banana you have ever eaten, but you say to your guide, "I'm having a terrific time." He replies, "There is more to come."

As you stand up, you feel the distance from your starting point growing larger and larger. You have a sinking feeling in your stomach and by now you start to wonder, "Did that leaf I chewed on make me sick? What will we do if something happens? How will we get out?" You start to fall behind and try to keep up, but your guide moves so much faster. You trip on roots that are along the trail. Your feet seem so heavy. At the next stop, an overlook, you confess that while you are having a good time, the walk is a bit difficult. "No problem," your guide says. "We will take it a little easier." You sit and look at the beauty before you. You rest, fuel up, and move on.

Because the pace has slowed, you are able to see things more clearly. You notice the wind in the trees and a chipmunk as it scurries across a fallen log. You see a squirrel as he keeps a close eye on you and the trail begins to narrow. Your guide warns you as he says, "Be careful. The next few feet is just dirt, held together by roots. There will be nothing underneath us." You shake your head, confident that you will be OK. Curious, you stomp on the ground and it indeed does sound hollow, leading you to believe that there is nothing below you. You guide says, "Be careful. You don't want to fall."

After several drops and climbs in elevation, you finally reach your destination. You hear it vaguely in the distance, but wonder if it is simply the wind again. Your mind is weak, and your muscles are even weaker, but the feeling is exhilarating as your guide says, "We are almost there." You are mad at him and yourself for going on this trip. Why would anyone in his right mind want to sweat and walk for three hours? As you round the corner, the sound is loud yet calming. You see a mist in the distance, and as you walk to the waterfall, the steps are surprisingly easy. Each step to this point has been a struggle, but now, with the goal in sight, you are able to keep up with your guide.

This illustration parallels perfectly your job as a parent. A guide on a trail must ensure that those who trust him do and know certain things, but realizes other hikers may not know everything. How can they? They may have never had experience on that trail. Not on a particular trail or any trail for that matter. With this in mind, a good guide will not belittle another hiker for not knowing something. He will not laugh. He will be patient. He will give other hikers what they need to survive. Doing anything else will only compromise the trip. It will make enemies out of friends, and it will make the journey more treacherous because each person depends on the other. Even the most experienced hiker (parent) can get injured along the way.

A model shows his child an example; a mentor joins with his child to ensure that he grows through experiences in life; and a guide must make 100% sure that his child learns and does certain things. Otherwise, as an inexperienced hiker on a trail without a guide, tragedy may strike.

Parenting Styles

Although I have developed various roles of the parent here, actually three types of parenting styles describe how you can interact with your children. Two of these are no good for your child when used exclusively, and the third is what you should be striving for as a parent.

During the early 1960s, psychologist Diana Baumrind conducted a study on more than 100 preschool-age children (Baumrind, 1967). Using various methods, she identified four important dimensions of parenting:[1]

- Disciplinary strategies
- Warmth and nurturance
- Communication styles
- Expectations of maturity and control

Based on these dimensions, Baumrind suggested that most parents utilize one of three different parenting styles.

Consider a child who is basically a blank slate. He does have some personality characteristics that cannot be changed. My son is naturally a caring person. He has some self-serving tendencies, but a natural sense of empathy is obvious. Your child may be extremely competitive or outgoing. She may be more reserved and inclined to think things through than react on impulse. Whatever the case, your child is an open vase that needs to have things put into it. Your child's personality serves only as a coat rack to hang philosophies that will make your child into the person he will someday become and the husband your daughter-in-law will respect, or the mother your grandchildren will adore. As a parent, you have been given the charge to shape your child and through your parenting style you can do this.

Permissive

The first form of parenting is known as permissive parenting. Possibly no parent would admit doing this, but we often lie to ourselves. Just how permissive/passive with your child are you?

A permissive parent interacts with his/her child yet fails to give clear boundaries, rules, or guidelines. Such a parent acts more like friends, priding themselves on being able to talk to their children, yet without the other task of directing a child in his/her behavior. This ridiculous notion comes from the idea of self-discovery. Allow a child to become who he wants to be, and he will be happier and healthier. Spawned from the free-wheeling philosophies of the 1960s, this style is a reaction by some who were forced to do and believe certain things by their authoritarian parents. More on this later.

Passive parenting believes that your child knows what is best. This has a slight degree of truth, but only as it relates to a child's personal interests. Do not push your child to be something he is not. He will deny your directives just because he can. Your child is smart? Athletic? Maybe you were. What is your child's talent, and are you sacrificing it to make him/her into something he or she is not? Are you pushing him in the wrong direction for his natural talents and abilities? Stop. This can be a good time to help him see who he can be for this world. He will figure it out himself eventually, and if he doesn't, he will be miserable his entire life. Don't let this happen. Encourage what your child loves.

Remember, this is primarily about your relationship with him. So, a good level of passivity is welcomed here, but it has more to do with your role as a mentor leading your child into discovery. However, your role as a guide says, "I must ensure that my child does x." Passive parenting would never allow this to happen.

Passive parenting of your teen believes that most categorical teen behavior should just be accepted. Things like staying in their rooms, constantly talking on the phone, being sexually active, and having a bad attitude are all labeled as "normal." They are. You cannot expect teens to act like an adult. They are going to be loud and obnoxious. They are going to chew with their mouths open and stink regularly.

Although all teens exhibit at least one or two of these behaviors, it should not deter you, the parent, from ensuring that your child does something else. I told a middle school client of mine (and her parents) that I was not too worried that she was constantly on the phone. Saying that she should not be on the phone or be in her room ever is too much to ask. They do need a social life. What bothered me was all the things her behavior was replacing. This is the point. When she is in her room eating, she is not at the dinner table. When she is talking on the phone for three hours every evening, she is not talking to her family. When she is watching television in her room, she is not playing games with the family.

Does your teen do something that bothers you, but you have chosen to passively ignore it? Does he stay by himself? Does he watch shows you do not approve of? Does he constantly miss curfew? If you are turning a blind eye to this, why? Probably because it is just easier. You figured, he is not hurting himself and *teens do that sort of thing* so it must be OK. After all, there is peace in the home. If you accept this notion, you are neglecting your responsibility as a parent and handing the job of affecting your son or daughter to his school, his friends, and whatever he happens to find on the internet while behind closed doors. Teen behavior is "normal," but it cannot be accepted as what is best.

Do not take yourself out of the equation but make yourself a part of it. I have heard parents say that they allow their kids' friends to their house all the time because they can keep an eye on them. This is genius parenting. You are in your child's world in such a way that both of you are comfortable with it.

Authoritarian

The second style of parenting is known as authoritarian. Parents are of course the authority, but take this idea too far and you have an unhappy home. Authoritarian parents expect their children to follow the strict rules of the home and if this is not done, punishment typically results. "Because I said so" is often the reason given, and high demands placed on the children are the norm.

This may not sound all that bad, but another characteristic of authoritarian parenting is that they are not responsive to their children. Structure and discipline should be the name of the game in everyone's homes but never at the expense of your child's intellectual, emotional, and spiritual growth. Nothing is quite as maddening as not knowing the reason for a rule. According to Baumrind, these parents "are obedience—and status-oriented, and expect their orders to be obeyed without explanation" (1991).[1] Many chances for bonding with your child are missed when walking the line is seen as more important.

Some would work to use passages that speak of physical punishment and of rule-following to advocate for this style of parenting. However, I do not see that this is how Jesus ministered at all.

Add in the fact that Christian parents are working to pass on their faith to their children. In Samuel 2:17, we learn this about Eli's sons, "Thus the sin of the young men was very great before the Lord, for the men despised the offering of the Lord." Why do children despise the teaching of the Lord today?

Democratic

Also known as authoritative, in this style of parenting parents set rules that their children are expected to follow, yet they are more responsive to their children and willing to listen to questions. When children fail to meet the expectations, these parents are more nurturing and forgiving than punishing. Baumrind suggests that these parents "monitor and impart clear standards for their children's conduct." They are:

- Assertive, not Intrusive
- Restrictive, not Confining
- Supportive, not Punitive

In essence, the authoritative style of parenting mixes the openness of the permissive style with the directness of authoritarian.

The Impact of Parenting Styles

In addition to Baumrind's initial study of 100 preschool children, researchers have conducted other studies that illustrate the impact of parenting styles on children. In general, authoritarian produces children who are obedient and hard working, but they rank lower in happiness, social competence, and self-esteem. Authoritive parenting tends to result in children who are happy, capable, and successful. "Permissive parenting often results in children who rank low in happiness and self-regulation. These children are more likely to experience problems with authority and tend to perform poorly in school."[2]

Bring Them Up

Ephesians 6:4: Paul says, "Fathers, do not provoke your children to anger, but bring them up in the discipline and instruction of the Lord." This verse encapsulates the democratic style of parenting. Jesus loved His disciples and showed them reasons for the rules He was giving them. He showed them how to act and how to be. He interacted with them and genuinely gave them good direction all the while loving them despite their imperfections.

As you learn how to be a better parent through this study and others, you must make decisions confidently. Parents, afraid to be push-overs, rule their children with an iron fist. Their desire to be dictator moves them into a position where they are unable to converse with their children. The disciples thought Jesus was in such a position and who wouldn't? He was healing people. He was God's Son. His wisdom surpassed anyone before or after Him. Why would Jesus need to squabble with a bunch of children who were seen as third class citizens in those days? But He saw their value. "But Jesus called for them, saying, 'Permit the children to come to Me, and do not hinder them, for the kingdom of God belongs to such as these'" (Luke 18:16). Jesus knew that children were a great part of His ministry.

Pray that you will have confidence in your parenting. As a guide, you must ensure that your child learns self-denial, a good work ethic, empathy, responsibility, and other characteristics that parents seem to overlook.

Larry Winget, in his book, *Your Kids Are Your Own Fault*, goes on a 272-page tirade about why your kids' mess-ups are yours, and he is right. Although children are born with some things, plenty of other things a child is not. Being rude, inconsiderate, ungrateful, sexually active, materialistic, jealous, contentious, angry and a drunk are real problems that a parent can stop from happening all together or fix if the child gets into them.

In 1 Samuel 2-4, we find a clear illustration of a struggling parent. Eli, a priest of the Lord at Shiloh, has two sons, Hophni and Phinehas (priests themselves) that sound a lot like boys today and maybe even your own son. Verse 12 of chapter two says, "Now the sons of Eli were worthless men . . . ." Why is this? Some have suggested that Eli was a passive type of parent although he did try to step in at least once. He had heard they were engaging in sexual relations with prostitutes. He, as a worried father says,

> "Why do you do such things, the evil things that I hear from all these people? No, my sons; for the report is not good which I hear the Lord's people circulating. If one man sins against another, God will mediate for him; but if a man sins against the Lord, who can intercede for him?" (1 Samuel 2:23-25).

God said He would judge Eli's house, ". . . for the iniquity which he knew, because his sons brought a curse on themselves and he did not rebuke them" (1 Samuel 3:13).

At least from what we know here, Eli was a passive parent.[2] Why would a parent then and today not rebuke his children? Maybe he was afraid of alienating his children from him. Some parents are so unsure of their parenting skills that they monitor their effectiveness by their child's happiness. If your child is not somewhat unhappy, you are not doing something right. A child is constantly working to get what he wants, and you as a parent must ensure that he gets what he *needs*. This is going to cause some strife.

Probably the saddest part of Eli's story is that his sons, ". . . did not know the Lord" (2:12). Are you telling me that the sons of a priest, who were priests themselves, did not know God? This happens a lot. Parents involved in ministry and who, in general, raise their children in a strict Christian home, are not guaranteed that their children will remain faithful.

Some might say that the answer to this is a more authoritarian style of parenting to keep them under your thumb so they will follow God. Good Christian parenting is a clear use of the democratic style. A parent must do things to make his child do the right things in regard to faith development. All people, at some point in their lives, would rather stay at home than get up and go to worship. It is the parent that keeps the child going. Through this experience, a child is taught the importance of faith in their lives. If a child is not brought up in the faith, he/she will follow whatever comes down the road. A parent who believes his/her way of living is right should pass this same belief system on to the children.

However, this authoritarian style approach should slowly fade. As the parent teaches Jesus' importance and value in one's life, the child sees this and adopts the belief as his own.

Conclusion

For those who want to have happy children, they forget to make them into good people. Leave it to Granny and Pa to make your kids happy. You are to make them responsible Christians. When they get home, you can be the loving guide they need long-term. This involves being in your child's life.

We cannot expect to live our daily lives that involve so much and expect to get great returns on our children without being involved. They are not made this way. They must be made through experiences with us. This comes with difficult moments, since your child may fight you every step of the way. But there are also joyous triumphs. By having this realistic view, parents can better handle the responsibility.

Questions for Discussion

1. A parent must ensure that his/her child learns certain things. What things do you believe are most important?

2. What are the positive parts of each of the parenting styles?

3. What parenting style did your parents employ and how does this affect your own parenting?

Notes

1. http://psychology.about.com/od/developmentalpsychology/a/parenting-style.htm
2. Dr. Paul Chappel, http://thebaptistvoice.com/categories/student-ministry/pitfalls-passive-parents

CHAPTER 8

Lessons Your Child Must Learn

In our country, parents have the right to raise their children as they see fit. We can be very thankful for this since it means that Christian parents can raise their children as Christians. However, there is a darker side to what goes on in homes today. They are not all peaceful, they are not all happy, and they are not all raising a healthy group of people for the next generation. While some children worry that they have to wait in line at a restaurant for 30 minutes, others worry that there will be no food at home. While some children worry that they will not get to watch shows on the Disney Channel that they have seen countless times, others worry that they will receive a harsh beating for a dirty sink.

The summer of 2012 proved trying for a fifteen-year-old girl in Butler, Georgia. She had been adopted around 2007, and home-schooled in a house about eighty-five miles south of Atlanta. The girl told investigators that she would spend as much as six days at a time in a chicken coop with a dog's shock collar around her neck as punishment for things like failing to do her school work. This had been going on for the past two years. "It was just big enough to sit in," one of the investigators told Fox News. [1]

In September of 2004, in my hometown of Lebanon, TN, a 15-year-old boy was found emaciated—weighing just 49 pounds—and chained to a bed wearing only a diaper that he had to change himself. Detective Scott Massey said, "In fourteen years, it was the most horrible case of child abuse ever." The parents, James Osborne III and his wife, Christie, had three other children ages 8, 6, and 5 who all seemed to be in good health. They were also removed from the home. [2]

When the boy arrived at the ER, he ate four plates of food. He was chained by his ankle to the frame of his bed for hours, and sometimes days, police said. When asked why this was done, Massey said, "(His Step-) mom says he's a troublemaker." Both the father and stepmother had keys to his bindings on their key rings. The abuse had gone on for months.

"The father told us he'd leave for work in the morning with the child chained to the bed," Massey said. "He'd get home, [the boy would] still be chained to the bed. He'd come home, unchain him, [let him] use the bathroom and tell him, 'Go back and chain yourself up before Mom finds out I let you go.'"

While these examples are extreme, it shows how parents do misuse their power. It also illustrates the level of power a parent possesses, and gives heed to the importance of how we must use it appropriately to say the least. However, there is an opposite side to the Nightmare Parent scenario.

In January 2007, AirTran Airways removed a Massachusetts couple from a flight after their crying three-year-old daughter refused to take her seat before takeoff. AirTran officials said they followed Federal Aviation Administration rules that children age 2 and above must have their own seat and be wearing a seat belt upon takeoff. [3]

"The flight was already delayed fifteen minutes and in fairness to the other one hundred twelve passengers on the plane, the crew made an operational decision to remove the family," AirTran spokeswoman Judy Graham-Weaver said. Julie and Gerry Kulesza, who were headed home to Boston on January 14 from Fort Myers, said they just needed a little more time to calm their daughter, Elly.

The crew-members were impatient you say? Three-year-olds are going to cry? Your heart bleeds for the mother who says, "We weren't given an opportunity to hold her, console her or anything." I agree that these were some of my original reactions as I have been the brunt of childless buffoons who have no idea what it means to raise a child. They are very difficult. However, how do you feel knowing that the little girl was climbing under the seat and hitting the parents? A grumpy child is one thing, but a child who obviously had control of this situation is an entirely different matter. I have heard parents say, "I can't get my child out of bed." I would just as soon cut off my right arm as to admit that I can't get my children to do something.

LZ Granderson, a CNN Contributor, said it this way in a response to the Air Tran incident.

If you're the kind of parent who allows your five-year-old to run rampant in public places like restaurants, I have what could be some rather disturbing news for you. I do not love your child. The rest of the country does not love your child either. And the reason why we're staring at you every other bite is not because we're acknowledging some sort of mutual understanding that kids will be kids, but rather we want to kill you for letting your brat ruin our dinner, our plane ride, and our trip to the grocery store.

Or the other adult-oriented establishments you've unilaterally decided will serve as an extension of your toddler's playpen because you lack the fortitude to properly discipline them, in public and at home.

And we know you don't discipline them at home because you don't possess "the look." If you had "the look," you wouldn't need to say "sit down" a thousand times.

If you had "the look," you wouldn't need to say much of anything at all. But this nonverbal cue needs to be introduced early and reinforced diligently with consequences for transgressions, just like potty training. And whenever a kid throws a temper tantrum in the middle of the shopping mall, it's just as bad as his soiling his pants to spite his parents, and it stinks just as much.

I have seen a small child slap her mother in the face with an open hand, only to be met with "Honey, don't hit Mommy." I have seen kids tell their parents "Shut up" and "Leave me alone" at the top of their lungs—and they are not put in check. I shake my head knowing it's only going to get worse from here.[4]

Granderson is exactly right. The battles parents face with their teens begin long before they ever hit their thirteenth year. You must raise a teen when he is three. You must raise an adult when he is five. You must not excuse bad behavior. It is your child's only chance to be a productive adult and hopefully a faithful Christian.

In Houston, Texas, the police department has repeatedly issued a leaflet entitled, "Twelve Rules for Raising Delinquent Children."[5]

1. Begin with infancy to give the child everything he wants. In this way he will grow up to believe the world owes him a living.
2. When he picks up bad words, laugh at him. This will make him think he's cute. It will also encourage him to pick up "cuter phrases" that

will blow off the top of your head later.

3. Never give him any spiritual training. Wait until he is 21, and then let him "decide for himself."

4. Avoid the use of the word "wrong." It may develop a guilt complex. This will condition him to believe later when he is arrested for stealing a car that society is against him and he is being persecuted.

5. Pick up everything he leaves lying around—books, shoes, clothes. Do everything for him so that he will be experienced in throwing all responsibility on others. Your future daughter-in-law will especially appreciate this.

6. Let him read any printed matter he can get his hands on. Be careful that the silverware and drinking glasses are sterilized, but don't worry about his mind feasting on garbage.

7. Quarrel frequently with your spouse in the presence of your children. In this way they will not be too shocked when the home is broken up later.

8. Give the child all the spending money he wants. Never let him earn his. Why should he have things as tough as you did?

9. Satisfy his every craving for food, drink, and comfort. See that every sensual desire is gratified. Denial may lead to harmful frustration.

10. Take his side against neighbors, teachers, and policemen. After all, they are prejudiced against your child.

11. When he gets into real trouble, apologize to yourself by saying, "I never could do anything with him!"

12. Prepare yourself for a life of grief. You'll surely have it.

Your children are being shaped by every experience they have in their home your home. How are you, the parent, the guide, shaping them.

Right vs. Wrong

It would be easier if our kids simply knew how to act. If they were born with some sort of trait that helped them to see what they should/should not do. Instead, they actually lack the ability to think logically about what their actions will result in. This is lacking in them biologically because their brain is still developing, but also because they have not experienced life as adults have. They do not know what works and what does not. They need someone to guide them.

Galatians 3 tells us why we needed the Law of Moses. It seems kind of redundant does it not? God establishes a pattern for living and then sends Jesus to establish a new law? Why not just send Jesus the first time? Galatians 3:19 says we received the law because of sinfulness. First Timothy 1:8-9a says, "But we know that the Law is good, if one uses it lawfully, realizing the fact that law is not made for a righteous person, but for those who are lawless and rebellious . . . ." We needed the old law to teach us right from wrong. A pattern of behavior had to be experienced by people so they would be able to say, "This is right and this is wrong." Our society has gone too far in a direction that totally leaves this type of dialogue out of the lives of our children. It is the cause of many of our problems today, even those problems in our homes. A child must be taught what he should and should not do. Parents can be extremely weak on this matter and thereby do their children much harm.

When discussing what parents want their children to be, many will point to people like a doctor, a pro-sports star, or someone else who is notably successful. However, when asked what we want our children to be, should we not answer, "a good person," one we can be proud of because of their character. This is the answer many parents rush in with, "Oh, well, yeah, of course." Although we want our children to be successful in their careers, we can get a great deal more longevity if we teach them how to be good people, and how to be good Christians. We must not simply teach them the stories, but rather we must teach them the life of a Christian.

If You Don't, Who Will?

Deuteronomy chapter 6 does a phenomenal job of telling us how to raise a child of God. The key is establishing this type of mindset in the 21st century Christian family where sacrifice, self-denial or going against the norm is not always convenient or popular. Instead of standing out, most Christians wish to blend in to the world so as not to allow their beliefs to alienate them from those they see at work and on the soccer field.

The first three verses tell us that if we follow God, we will prosper. We are comfortable with this notion. I can follow God. No problem. It gets a bit more detailed than this. Verses four and five say to "love the Lord your God with all your heart and with all your soul and with all your might." We condone this too. We can love God. We might not think of this exactly, but loving God and following God are things we can tell ourselves we are doing in our homes and when we attend worship. Verses six through nine get a little more into our lives.

> "These words, which I am commanding you today, shall be on your heart. You shall teach them diligently to your sons and shall talk of them when you sit in your house and when you walk by the way and when you lie down and when you rise up. You shall bind them as a sign on your hand and they shall be as frontals on your forehead. You shall write them on the doorposts of your house and on your gates."

God wants all of us, but we are in such a blessed country, and our children have more than any other generation before them. It would be so easy for us to, "forget the Lord" as verse twelve warns the children of Israel. No parent wants his or her child to forget God as they grow and when they leave home. (Read Flavil Yeakley's work entitled, *Why They Left: Listening to Those Who Have Left Churches of Christ* for more information.)

Having a plan to reach our children, while not fail proof, is important in working to establish in them a faith that will last. What would you say if your son were to ask you what verse 20 suggests? "What *do* the testimonies and the statutes and the judgments *mean* which the Lord our God commanded you?" What will you tell him about your faith? The Israelites had a strong testimony. They were slaves in Egypt, and God did a great deal to bring them out of that bondage. What is your story? What do you teach your child about your faith? What has God done for you? You must be purposeful in your teaching if you are to raise godly children. A good place to start is the fruit of the Spirit.

Your Child Is Flesh

In our over-abundant society, it is easy to teach fleshly desires as described in Galatians 5. Immorality, impurity, sensuality are in vogue with today's youth. Facebook posts by teen-oriented groups are highly sexual, and your teen may be following these very groups, getting fed a steady stream of temptation. Idolatry is easy as every afternoon 15 year-old boys masterfully maneuver through digital worlds. I do not think your child will become a sorcerer if he reads *Harry Potter*, but I do know that if he is not given a guiding philosophy for his life (i.e. Christianity), the dark arts could be a place he looks.

Are your children constantly arguing? This is nothing more than enmities, strife, and jealousy. Does your child say he has an anger problem (outbursts of anger)? Set him straight by explaining that he has an anger *control* problem that he needs to get started on. Are your children constantly fighting with you (disputes, dissensions, factions, envying)? If so, it might be because they are on their way to a life of drunkenness and carousing. Succumbing to these natural desires is simple. If parents do not consciously combat these, their children will not know any other way to live.

Although you may not be teaching these negative behaviors directly, what are you purposefully teaching? What are you making sure your child knows and does? The flesh that Paul struggled with in Romans 7 is the same your child (even your little five-year-old) currently battles. "For we know that the Law is spiritual, but I am of flesh, sold into bondage to sin" (Romans 7:14). The difference is, your child may not be hating the fact that he gives in to the flesh as Paul mentions in verse 15. Although we are not born evil, we are born flesh. If one of the most admired apostles of the first century struggled, you had better believe that your child is struggling. Or, he may not be struggling at all if he is not taught otherwise. He may be swimming in the flesh and loving it.

When you teach your child that some things are wrong and that some things are right, you give him a code to live by. You teach him guilt, which is a very powerful emotion that can give him some direction. This is much better than the terribly misguided feelings developed over time. Hopefully through what you teach, his feelings will tell him the right thing to do.

Fruits of the Spirit

This teaching begins early on. You cannot think that the way you raise your three-year-old will have no consequences when he is thirteen. If you are lenient now, he will expect it later. If you do not speak to him now, do not expect to speak to him easily when he is running out the door to meet up with some friends. Every day you take with your child is a step toward a grown individual you will want to have a relationship with later. The best way to do this is to help your child grow into an adult. Too many children just grow up. We must raise them, and a good guide is the fruit of the Spirit.

The first fruit identified in Galatians 5 is love, and the best place to learn about this is 1 Corinthians 13. There are some concepts that overlap between love and the fruit of the spirit so let's focus on those that differ. First, love is not jealous, does not brag, is not arrogant and does not act unbecomingly. These are particularly useful when dealing with sibling rivalry that will happen. When it does, remind your children that they are to be happy for the successes of their brother or sister. Help them find the good feeling that can come from not being jealous or arrogant. The flesh says to push people down so I can build myself up, but Jesus said that if we are to be first, we must be last. This is something your child will not learn on his own, but he can still become a champion if you help him.

Second, love does not seek its own, is not provoked, and does not take into account a wrong *suffered*. I believe a good word that can be used for all of love but especially this section, is "empathy"—the ability to think of others before oneself. It is not apathy which is a lack of caring, something many teens have, nor is it sympathy where I know intellectually how someone must feel. Instead, empathy is when I have a deep awareness of how someone must feel. I can actually feel it along with the one hurting. This awareness motivates me to do right. Jesus said to treat others the way we want to be treated. Then we understand how they must feel.

Empathy can be difficult to teach. You cannot give your child the definition and expect him to be able to practice it. One way to ensure that empathy is developed in your child is to have him reflect on how he would feel were someone to treat him the same as he treats others. Also, experiencing life-changing events like mission trips or working at a mission can help a child see outside himself and work with the idea of what someone else must feel.

Third, love does not rejoice in unrighteousness, but rejoices with the truth. You must help your child see the wisdom found in Scripture. Because we have all that we could ever want materially in this world, it is very easy to allow these things to rule us much as the rich young ruler did. He had done so much to be religious, but was unwilling to leave behind everything. This takes some maturity on the part of a young person, but you must teach and model this in your own life. Otherwise, your child will rejoice with falsehoods and the wisdom of man.

Finally, love bears all things, believes all things, hopes all things, endures all things. This is a lesson in marital commitment. If your child is to meet someone and remain with that one forever, you must teach your child that love is commitment.

The fruit of the Spirit continues with joy. We all want our children to be happy. We want them to experience things like a waterfall, a hug, and good devotional singing, knowing that happiness does not have to come from things, but rather that it can come from within us because we see the beauty of God all around us.

Your child must also learn peace. Many a tortured soul has experienced a lack of peace, and a lack of knowledge of what Philippians 4:6-7 says:

> "Be anxious for nothing, but in everything by prayer and supplication with thanksgiving let your requests be made known to God. And the peace of God, which surpasses all comprehension, will guard your hearts and your minds in Christ Jesus."

Many people experience anxiety, but no other group has more of it than today's youth. They are running to the limits of human capacity with busy schedules. But a greater cause of their anxiety is a lack of inner peace, peace that says, "I am loved by my parents, I am loved by my heavenly Father and I can rest assured that were I to die today, I would live forever." If we are to teach today's youth to survive in an ever-changing and sinful world, they must know peace.

Patience follows peace in this passage, but also in practice. You must teach your child to wait and to know that things do not move on her time. This will help her to think of others and sit quietly with her thoughts, something that kids are beginning to do less and less. Being patient and waiting is a good way to spend time with a good friend; him or herself. Teach your child this.

Kindness, goodness, faithfulness, and gentleness are all easy to recognize as desirable traits for a child, but how do you teach them or help your child experience them. Show him what it means to be kind. If he is an aggressive child, he can take up for others. If he says he is going to do something, help him reach that goal (faithfulness). He does not have to be mean to get his way, and by being a friend to others, he will get many friends himself.

Self-control is the final fruit of the Spirit, and it is a good one to cap off the list. If a child knows the deeds of the flesh, he can stay away from them. However, if he lacks self-control, he may simply find ways to delve into those things he knows he should stay away from. How can you teach self-control? Say "no" regularly to your child. Tell him or her why you say "no" and help each one understand that you are not being mean, but that you want them to grow with character traits that matter. Read about the fruit of the Spirit at night. The deeds of the flesh will be found out soon enough, but don't let the fruit of the Spirit be a lesson not learned until summer camp the sophomore year. Proverbs 29:15B says, ". . . a child who gets his own way brings shame to his mother." Teach him self-control for his benefit and for yours.

Conclusion

What type of life are you fashioning for your child? Is it one where they will flourish when they leave or one where they will be afraid to go out into the world alone? Is it one that is grounded in biblical principles? If you want your child to carry them with him out the door, you must equip him with the knowledge of the fruit of the Spirit and the dangers of the flesh. Then, the armor of God will not be so difficult to put on.

Questions for Discussion

1. What are the most important lessons your child must learn in and outside of Christianity?

2. We are quick to ridicule other parents. What behaviors do you see in others that you can also see in yourself?

3. What fleshly desires do children and teens give in to and what biblical principles can help them combat these sins?

Notes

1. http://www.foxnews.com/us/2012/07/12/parents-accused-locking-girl-in-chicken-coop-forcing-her-to-wear-shock-collar/

2. http://abcnews.go.com/US/story?id=96669&page=1#.UKZqYaXEAm8

3. http://www.msnbc.msn.com/id/16773655/ns/travel-news/t/airline-defends-removing-family-flight/#.UKaE56XEAm8

4. http://articles.cnn.com/2011-07-05/opinion/granderson.bratty.kids_1_airtran-flight-kid-free-tantrum?_s=PM:OPINION

5. http://www.snopes.com/glurge/12rules.asp

CHAPTER 9

The Boy and Girl Factors

The current generations of parents, generation X and Y have witnessed America's gender shift away from a male-dominated society to one where women have equal opportunity. The girls do not know what their mothers and grandmothers endured so that they could work for equal pay and even vote. The children of those parents (known as millenials) will never know of the inequality perpetrated on the American woman by laws that should have served to protect them. We most assuredly have come a long way.

Even though our progress toward equality has led us in a good direction, we must never lose sight of the fact that men and women are different. By not acknowledging this fact, you risk not maximizing your children's potential. This is something the suffragist league would not have you do to your daughter or to your son. May we always respect each child's differences and not assume that because he is a boy, he will play with trucks or that because she is a girl, she should not like math. Imposing stereotypes is harmful and much different than acknowledging the characteristics that make each gender unique, and that manifest themselves in children through various means. I will be making general statements in this chapter, but I do recognize that there are exceptions to every rule. However, I want to speak in general terms here with the hopes that it will apply to the preponderance of boys and girls.

Being a Boy Is a Liability

When people use the phrase, "when I was in school," it makes them sound senile and out of touch with reality. But not that long ago, I was actually in high school. Nineteen years ago; that was a long time ago, but the transition of my graduating class (1995) was a part of changed campuses all over our country. My junior and senior years began with shootings in public schools.

Gang affiliated boys were taking guns to school for defense and for retribution. February of 1996 (my freshman year at Freed-Hardeman University) ensured that the phrase, "mass school shootings," would become a normal part of our lexicon.

Feb. 2, 1996 - Moses Lake, WA - Two students and one teacher killed, one other wounded when 14-year-old Barry Loukaitis opened fire on his algebra class.

Oct. 1, 1997 - Pearl, MS. - Two students killed and seven wounded by Luke Woodham, 16, who was also accused of killing his mother. He and his friends were said to be outcasts who worshiped Satan.

Dec. 1, 1997 - West Paducah, KY - Three students killed, five wounded by Michael Carneal, 14, as they participated in a prayer circle at Heath High School.

March 24, 1998 - Jonesboro, AK - Four students and one teacher killed, 10 others wounded outside as Westside Middle School emptied during a false fire alarm. Mitchell Johnson, 13, and Andrew Golden, 11, shot at their classmates and teachers from the woods.

April 20, 1999 - Littleton, CO - Fourteen students (including killers) and one teacher killed, 23 others wounded at Columbine High School in the nation's deadliest school shooting. Eric Harris, 18, and Dylan Klebold, 17, had plotted for a year to kill at least 500 and blow up their school. At the end of their hour-long rampage, they turned their guns on themselves.[1]

These tragedies were committed by my gender; by my race. The others that followed over the ensuing twenty years have led to drastic changes on how we view bullying, but it has also cast a shadow on characteristics predominantly in males.

The School System

When I was in school, boys got up early to go hunting during deer season. They would then drive their trophy to school with the gun in the rack on the back windshield. Today, a boy who farms with his dad for a living can get suspended for having a box cutter in the package in his locked truck. If we had tolerance, we couldn't call it "Zero Tolerance." I suppose, but the phrase "zero common sense" seems to apply here too.

Any time a boy draws a skull or a gun at school, he is sent to the principal.

I know, because I have to look into it. "Are you thinking about killing yourself? Someone else? Do you want to bring a gun to school? Do you have access to a gun?" I don't like doing this, but I also do not want to be another statistic. It is the world we live in now.

Unfortunately aggressiveness (a desire for adventure and raw male energy) is demonized for the sake of the ideal student; a boy who sits quietly in his chair and listens. The opposite of this is often labeled a troublemaker, or teachers assume he does not want to learn and is only there to waste their time. Society has truly lost its way when we medicate a boy for being a boy, yet encourage him if he thinks he's a girl.

Our current educational style is made for girls. They can sit, study, and do as they are told. Some boys have the capacity for this (my son does), but many do not. Thank goodness for teachers like my wife who have boys and girls constantly on the move through an interactive learning environment.

Your son is extremely bright, loves to read, did well in school at one time, but has either suddenly or gradually decided he does not care whether he gets an A or an F. You lecture and you punish, but nothing seems to motivate him. In his book, *Boys Adrift*, Leonard Sax looks at the epidemic of "underachieving boys and unmotivated young men." He gets at the heart of why our boys are failing.[2]

Your son is smart but can't sit still in class. Has anyone suggested medication or an ADHD diagnosis? Possibly, and you may have even researched it yourself. Your son may not be the problem, but it may be that you and his teacher are asking your son to do something he is not *developmentally* ready to do.

The thrust of Sax's book is that boys do not seem to care about much. One 14 year-old son told his mother, "Girls care about getting good grades. Geeks care about grades. Normal guys do not care about grades." We should not think that this is a boy just being a boy. Sax references Tom Sawyer and Ferris Bueller who never had any interest in school. They did however pursue interests and worked toward their own schemes. Some boys today lack motivation and want to reach "guyhood" by being as successful as possible at doing *nothing*.

In 2007, a study done by the National Institute of Mental Health supported other studies reporting that the language areas of the brain in many five-year-old boys look like the language areas of the brain of the average three-and-a-half-year-old girl.[3] Your son has been struggling for a few years and finally says mid-elementary, "I hate school." He may be attempting something his brain is not ready to do. Why shouldn't he hate it?

In another fundamental difference between boys and girls, girls have an innate desire to please the adults in their lives. The type of boys Sax discusses in his book do not have this desire. As we know, some boys work to please, but others want to anger the closest authority figure. Girls are more likely to see situations from the point of view of the adults in charge. Boys lack this depth of empathy. So, of course girls will do better in school and enjoy it more. From 1949 to 2006, boys enrolled in a four-year college dropped from 70 percent to 42 percent. More girls are going because of obvious changes in our culture, but fewer boys are in attendance.[4]

Not only are boys behind developmentally just because of their biology; certain school factors are unfriendly to boys. Over the past thirty years, many school districts have eliminated sports such as dodgeball, believing that such sports "reward violence." Competition has also been eliminated because it "alienates some kids from sports." Although we worry about the unathletic kids, we are losing those who thrive in such atmospheres. A boy with this persona may look at an environment void of competition and say, "Why bother?" Indeed!

Medication

Boys are designed to be playful, rambunctious and sometimes outright raunchy. These characteristics do not always fit into a school setting, and after many bouts with school personnel, bewildered parents go to their doctor to discuss an ADHD diagnosis. The parents may also be frustrated about his behavior at home. The boy begins a behavior modification regimen along with meds that will make it easier to control himself. The boy's teachers are relieved and the parents are pleased. He is doing much better in school, and this can be attributed directly to the doctor's visit. But what if there's more to this story?

ADHD has always been with us. In *The Adventures of Tom Sawyer*, we have an early example of what we would later term Attention Deficit Hyperactivity Disorder. But is it a disorder or is it simply boys being boys? Nobody would argue in Sawyer's time that he was doing anything out of the ordinary, but in a 21st century school, he certainly would not make it.

Some boys can sit for hours at a time and do their work as requested by the teacher. Others, however, can barely sit still for five minutes. Most classes are not designed for boys who absolutely must be active. However, it is a fact that if a hyperactive boy is to graduate in this day and age, he must receive some form of help or struggle his entire academic career and within his social circles. Medication can help in this struggle. Although medication is an aid, my hope is that through the strategies in this book, you will look to the medical industry as a last resort.

America is the most prescribed country in the world. What has led to this? First, we have made a tremendous shift from personal responsibility to third-party explanations. If something is wrong with a person, he/she is quick to blame his lousy parents, a sibling, a friend, drugs, alcohol, almost anything other than himself. Because he is a victim of outside circumstances, he must get outside help. Little if any thought is given to a person having or developing the strength to handle his own behavior.

In 2006, children in the U.S. were at least three times more likely to be taking psychiatric medications as compared with children in any European country. And our kids aren't just taking one pill. One-third of American children who are taking psychotropic meds are actually taking two to four others. A boy who is on Adderall for his ADHD may also be on Clonidine to control his outbursts and Prozac to stabilize his moods.[5] The result: a boy who conforms, but who is not developing inner strength to cope and control. These character traits should be developed in the home and at school with firm teachers and practical parents.

Three decades ago if a boy cursed his parents or spit at his teacher, people would say that he was a disobedient brat who was long due a spanking. Today, this behavior from a similar boy might prompt a trip to the pediatrician or child psychologist. It's no longer the fault of the parents or the boy who needs to learn self-control; instead he is an unfortunate soul with misfiring chemicals. What is wrong with him is the wrong question. Rather, you must ask what are you as the parent going to do to change his behavior? Most can learn to control themselves even without the assistance of medications. When the negative behavior pushes one way, it must meet with resistance from the parents.

The purpose of medication is to get your son to conform to the degree that he will be able to succeed in the pathway that the public school system has designated. But what if this medication keeps him from wanting to succeed? Will you have a 25 year-old living in your basement spending all his paycheck on video games? Maybe.

Professor William Carlezon and his colleagues at Harvard Medical School have reported that juvenile laboratory animals display a loss of drive when they mature after being given stimulant medications such as those used to treat boys with ADHD. These medications appear to impair lab animals by damaging the nucleus accumbens of the developing brain. Independent groups of researchers at the University of Michigan, the Medical University of South Carolina, the University of Pittsburgh, Brown University, as well as in Sweden, Italy and the Netherlands have arrived at similar conclusions. What's the point? Your boy may feel hungry. He just won't do anything about it.[6]

Thankfully, these adverse affects can be overcome by engaging your son in activities that interest him and by ensuring that he does have a degree of motivation to do something. Otherwise, there may be cause for concern. I have witnessed boys who are better for taking medication, but I have also seen boys who could benefit from other forms of interventions.

Video Games

What is excessive video-game play? The average boy spends more than 13 hours a week playing video games. Some experts say that 30 minutes to an hour should be the max, but this can be left up to the parent of course.[7] Video games can be a good diversion on long trips, and weekends are meant for more leisure time. In my experience, 40 minutes seems to be reasonable.

Here are some things to consider if you wonder whether your child is playing too much. Is he losing sleep? Are his grades dropping at school? Is he obsessed with playing? It has been proved that video games release dopamine (the pleasure chemical of the brain) in much the same way drugs release it. No wonder kids want to play so much; these games have addictive qualities. Therefore, game time must be seriously regulated, particularly because boys lose a sense of time when engrossed with a game. Three hours can actually feel like 30 minutes.

What is the correlation between boys who play and those who aren't contributing much to society or their own future? These are boys who care little about their grades, are content to live with their parents well into adulthood and have no interest in relationships that might lead to a family. In video games, boys are in control. They are tested at doing their best and are rewarded for their success. These are all things that typically drive boys to succeed in society, but if they are getting these rewards from games, why should they seek them elsewhere? Sax interviewed girls who said that boys would rather play games than pursue them. What?! Video games fill a void for boys, causing them to get all the fulfillment they need, but to what end? A high score?

Some proponents argue that video games make kids smarter and that they give the gamers faster hand/eye coordination. These are small payoffs for the amount of time squandered away at getting virtual points in a virtual world with virtual friends. Where is the real pay off? The Atlanta Braves are not calling because your son won the Virtual World Series. He may be quicker on the draw, but Sax states that it is only by two-hundredths of a second (0.02) – when compared to kids who don't play. It's not worth it.

Is he smarter? Hardly. He may be smarter at the video game, but the evidence does not support a cause and effect from games to school. In fact, "A series of studies over the past seven years has demonstrated clearly and unambiguously" that the more time your child spends playing video games, the less likely he is to do well in school at any level.[8] Furthermore, as researchers account for variables, the evidence becomes stronger.

Don't get me wrong. Some gaming is good. I play with my son, and we have a good time together. I even use it to exercise. The main point to ponder is, "Are games taking the place of other, more enriching activities?" Also, is the subject matter appropriate? Researchers at Yale University have reported that playing violent video games leads directly to "aggressive behavior . . . and decreases in helping behavior." Gamers also report fewer friends, depression, and heightened anxiety. Don't get scared just yet because these come from excessive play.[9]

As a parent, you must ask yourself whether your son is playing too much. If he doesn't care about school, wants to stay in all the time, and has few interests that can contribute to his future, it may be time to limit or completely take away the system. After all, will his life really be better if he continues playing?

Anger

While working with middle schoolers I hear a lot about how boys have "anger problems." For most, this is terribly inaccurate. The anger is not the problem, but rather it's the lack of anger control. As boys grow into their teen years, they experience high doses of testosterone. This causes emotions, especially anger, to run rampant. When provoked, boys may react in a highly emotional way causing parents and teachers to comment, "You have an anger problem." This assessment can be detrimental.

If you call it a problem, it may give the boy a weakened desire to control his behavior because there's apparently something wrong with him. There's a "problem." Getting angry and losing one's temper is not a sickness, but a natural part of growing up. The feelings that accompany this change can be very difficult, but not impossible to manage.

The best thing parents can do is listen at appropriate times. If you yell back or fire off a bunch of questions, this may serve to worsen the situation. Give him some time to cool down, and he may come to you on his own. If not, go to him and listen. Next, do not minimize his feelings. Telling him, "Well, that's just crazy," doesn't often help. His feelings may seem silly to you, but to him they are his life and are very real. Anger is often a secondary emotion used to express sadness or confusion. Don't give advice, but help by leading him to a proper view of the situation.

Anger does become a problem when there is no reasoning with the person at any state of their mood. They believe their actions are justified no matter who or what is hurt. This may call for a diagnosis like Oppositional Defiant Disorder (ODD), and work with a therapist may be necessary. Medication can also help. Please understand that diagnoses like ODD are used to conceptualize something so that professionals can work with the client. They should never be used as an excuse for a person's behavior.

There are some good reasons explaining why boys get mad. I listen as the twelve year old tells me about mom's escapades that led him to be put into foster care. I hold back my emotion as boy after boy shrugs his shoulders to the question, "Where's your dad?" Their despair haunts me as I hug my own son and pray that I don't fail as a father.

Without positive male figures or strong mothers, these boys are left to figure out manhood on their own. They have holes in their lives that they sadly fill with rage and hatred. I can't blame them for being mad. Many are physically and emotionally tormented by people who should love them. Boys need someone to show them how to control their anger, love their future wives, and care for their family. They don't need people who strap dog shock collars to their necks when they misbehave.

Girls

Do you have a double standard with your son and daughter? Would you let your 16-year-old son go out on a Saturday night, unknown as to his whereabouts? Would you allow your daughter? You may or may not allow both, but which are you more apprehensive about? Their personalities may play a part in your decision, but in general, most parents would feel more squeamish about allowing their daughters to go out. Is this a sexist double standard grounded in old-timey thinking? I don't think so. I believe it is a sexist double standard that has a proper place in raising teens.

Every teen is different, but you are going to be less inclined to worry about your 200-pound boy than you are your 110-pound girl. Let's face it, they have different needs. He may get a bloody nose from running his mouth, but the girl's situations are the stuff of nightmares. Boys could be in horrible scenarios such as going too fast and crashing, but give him the tools and he will hopefully not kill himself. Put a girl too far into some risky situations, and she may be unable to get out. Looking for acceptance, she may do more than smoke a cigarette. The boy, you have to protect from himself, but the girl, you must protect from others.

The world is a dangerous place for our daughters, and parents must defend them. What the world says makes girls happy, really doesn't, and the "nice guy" really isn't. Parents should listen to their guts, not their daughters' whining, the latest trends, or the magazine rack at Wal-Mart. To raise a self-respecting woman of integrity is much better than raising a spoiled princess who gets exploited because of her beauty and dad's bottomless wallet.

They Are at Risk; Even by Their Parents

We have discussed how boys can be lazy, and we can actually set them up that way by giving them other, more non-productive activities to engage in. Well, for our girls, the epidemic is a bit different. In his book, *Girls on the Edge*, Leonard Sax shows how the will to succeed causes girls pain and anguish as he discusses four factors that are driving our girls down a path of self-destruction. Some would term his observations old-fashioned, but it's hard to argue with his plainly stated research. Gender roles, when based on facts and figures, carry a great deal of weight. To be clear, different does not mean inferior as some may assume.[10]

The first factor is that of *sexual identity*.[11] The chapter consisted a lot of what I expected; the over-sexualization of young girls and the sexual empowerment movement has led many girls to be disempowered. If girls are not given the proper direction, their sexual identity will seek to be fulfilled in ways that will leave them dissatisfied, emotional wrecks. The world tells them to be sexual: that it's the only way they'll be accepted. You, as the parent, must notice this and protect your daughter.

The second factor he calls the *cyberbubble*.[12] In this chapter he discusses how social networking (ie Facebook, Twitter, etc.) has driven girls into their own unfulfilling worlds where they look for something and get a lot, but find nothing of substance. Parents whose girls are suffering because of this social cyber-world look for answers in prescriptions, when all that really needs to be done is limiting time online.

Thirdly, Sax discusses *obsessions*.[13] We expect a lot of our girls, and they work extremely hard at numerous activities. Because of the changes in our world these last fifty years, our girls have been given the green light to succeed with their talents. This is tremendous news. However, many go so far as to risk injury and well-being. How good is good enough? Because some girls and their parents don't know, they never quit. This is dangerous because it too leads down a path with no end. When Jesus told the woman at the well that if she drank from His water she would never thirst, He meant it, and He means it for our little girls today too.

The fourth factor, as in *Boys Adrift*, discusses *environmental toxins*.[14] Sax asks and answers questions that may still leave you wondering, but his facts make sense. Whatever you believe after reading about the dangerous chemicals in things like food and personal care products, something is going on when girls are hitting puberty at age eight. Can a man cause his daughter's puberty to delay until a more appropriate time? According to Sax, it is likely.

In the final portion of the book, Sax discusses your daughter's mind, body, and spirit in an unpretentious manner. I appreciate this, for it enables a person of any faith or creed to consider what they want for their daughter. His method for these final chapters will cause all parents to wonder on a level beyond sports and school, just what they are doing for their daughter's growth and development.

Dad Must Play His Crucial Part

Through her medical practice, Meg Meeker has seen the effects an absent or ineffective father figure can have in a girl's life. Depression, STD's, drug abuse, and eating disorders are but a few life-wrenching struggles girls experience in their teen years. Meeker explains that a father can curb these if he will only take an active role in his daughter's life; even in divorce situations.[15]

The world tells you not to hug your daughter. She will hug someone else, and it will likely be someone you do not approve of. Society tells you to give your daughter freedom, but as she is trying to figure out life on her own, her peers are influencing her for the worst. You say you can't talk to your daughter? Meeker suggests it's probably because her face is in a digital screen all the time and she does not know how to converse one-on-one. If you do not step in, the world will capture her and tell her she has to dress a certain way and act a certain way to be happy. This road leads to a fruitless dead end.

Conclusion

Boys have a great need to find themselves in this world. They want to know that they can accomplish great things whether seated at a desk, working in a kitchen, or being a stay-at-home dad. Help your son see his strengths and work to develop them so he can be the man God would have him be.

No one cares for your daughter the way you do. The clothing industry doesn't; the media doesn't and boys most certainly don't view your daughter as the precious being that she is. You must help your daughter see these segments of society for what they are. They do not have her best interests in mind. Only you do. Stand and protect her. She may be screaming all the way, but she'll thank you for it in the end.

Questions for Discussion

1. In what ways is it appropriate/not appropriate to treat your boy and girl child differently?

2. How can you encourage the appropriate behaviors in boys in order to help them grow into good Christian men?

3. How can you encourage the appropriate behaviors in girls in order to help them grow into good Christian women?

Notes

1. "Timeline of School and Mass Shootings" http://www.infoplease.com/ipa/A0777958.html

2. Sax, M.D., Ph.D., L. (2007). *Boys adrift: The five factors driving the growing epidemic of unmotivated boys and underachieving young men*. New York: Basic Books.

3. Ibid.

4. Ibid.

5. Ibid.

6. Ibid.

7. Brogaard, B. Computer games and brain development. Retrieved February 2012 from http://www.ehow.com/about_6653128_computer-games-brain-development.html.

8. Sax, M.D., Ph.D., L. (2007). *Boys adrift: The five factors driving the growing epidemic of unmotivated boys and underachieving young men.* New York: Basic Books.

9. Ibid.

10. Sax, M.D., Ph.D., L. (2011). *Girls on the Edge: The Four Factors Driving the New Crisis for Girls – Sexual Identity, the Cyberbubble, Obsessions & Environmental Toxins.* New York: Basic Books.

11. Ibid.

12. Ibid.

13. Ibid.

14. Sax, M.D., Ph.D., L. (2007). *Boys adrift: The five factors driving the growing epidemic of unmotivated boys and underachieving young men.* New York: Basic Books.

15. Meeker, Meg, M.D., (2006). *Stong Fathers, Strong Daughters.* Regnery Publishing; 1 edition (September 30, 2006)

Bibliography

1. "Timeline of School and Mass Shootings" http://www.infoplease.com/ipa/A0777958.html

2. Brogaard, B. Computer games and brain development. Retrieved February 2012 from http://www.ehow.com/about_6653128_computer-games-brain-development.html.

3. Chabris, C., Simons, D. (2010). *The Invisible Gorilla: How our intuitions deceive us.* New York: Broadway Books.

4. Collins, B. (2006). Dying to play. *PC Authority.* Retrieved January 2012 from http://www.google.com/url?sa=t&rct=j&q=dying%20to%20play%20barry%20collins%20olganon&source=web&cd=1&sqi=2&ved=0CB4QFjAA&url=http%3A%2F%2Fericeventwiki.wikispaces.com%2Ffile%2Fview%2FDying%2Bto%2Bplay.RTF&ei=VCM9T5OKKMrltgfevLXgBQ&usg=AFQjCNFiwZqDDyJywKPqkLCvsg0R7_SiPQ&sig2=yiZs_8ZbdEe0WHw87GZYCA

5. Darrall, S. (2011, November 27). Violent video games do make people more aggressive. Retrieved January 2012 from http://www.dailymail.co.uk/sciencetech/article-2066803/Violent-video-games-DO-make-people-aggressive.html.

6. Gentile, D.A., Anderson, C.A. (2003, October 16). Violent video games: The newest media violence hazard. Retrieved January 2012 from http://drdouglas.org/drdpdfs/106027_07.pdf.

7. Grace, J. (2006, January 24). Children are less able than they used to be. *Guardian.* p. 3.

8. Jansz, J. (2005) The Emotional Appeal of Violent Video Games for Adolescent Males. Retrieved January 2012 from http://onlinelibrary.wiley.com/doi/10.1111/j.1468-2885.2005.tb00334.x/abstract.

9. Kardaras, E. (2008, January 7). The Effects of video games on the brain. Retrieved January 2012 from http://serendip.brynmawr.edu/exchange/node/1742.

10. Meeker, Meg, M.D., (2006). *Strong Fathers, Strong Daughters.* Regnery Publishing; 1 edition (September 30, 2006)

11. Mori, A. (2002). *The Fear of game brain.* Japan: Japan Broadcast Publishing.

12. Parrott, Dr. L. (2000). *Helping the struggling adolescent: A guide to thirty-six common problems for counselors, pastors, and youth workers.* Grand Rapids, MI: Zondervan.

13. Rauh, S. Video game addiction no fun. Retrieved January 2012 from http://www.webmd.com/mental-health/features/video-game-addiction-no-fun.

14. Sax, M.D., Ph.D., L. (2007). *Boys Adrift: The five factors driving the growing epidemic of unmotivated boys and underachieving young men.* New York: Basic Books.

15. Sax, M.D., Ph.D., L. (2011). *Girls on the Edge: The Four Factors Driving the New Crisis for Girls – Sexual Identity, the Cyberbubble, Obsessions & Environmental Toxins.* New York: Basic Books.

16. Scheeres, S. (2001, December 5). The Quest to end game addiction. *Wired.* Retrieved January 2012 from http://www.wired.com/gaming/gamingreviews/news/2001/12/48479?currentPage=all

17. Steinburg, Scott. (2011, January 31). How video games can make you smarter. Retrieved January 2012 from http://articles.cnn.com/2011-01-31/tech/video.games.smarter.steinberg_1_video-games-interactive-simulations-digital-world?_s=PM:TECH.

18. Sundeta, J.S., Barlaugb, D.G., Torjussen, T.M. (2004). The End of the Flynn Effect? A study of secular trends in mean intelligence test scores of Norwegian conscripts during half a century, *Intelligence*, volume 32, pp 349-362.

19. Teasdale, T., Owen, D. (2005). A Long-Term Rise and Recent Decline in Intelligence Test Performance: The Flynn effect in reverse, *Personality and Individual Differences*, volume 39, pp 837-843.

20. Uhlmann, E., Swanson, J. (2004) Exposure to Violent Video Games Increases Automatic Aggressiveness, *Journal of Adolescence*, Volume 27, pp. 41-52.

CHAPTER 10

The Joys and Frustrations of Parenting

Parenting is fraught with joys and frustrations. Some of these are real and inherent in the job we signed up for. Because some of the frustrations are brought on by parental misadventure, some of the joys are regrettably missed. Parenting is an adventure, and life is no longer about you. It is about raising a human being that might change the world for the better. Some of the frustrations in parenting come from not understanding what to do. I have tried to address some of them. However, it's also about wishing things were different. Instead of wishing, we must be patient and work to shape our child into what we want them to be. It's hard because it's supposed to be hard, but through the trials the joys are that much brighter.

In 2004 within the span of about three months, Malita and I experienced several life-altering events. Our son Mason announced his pending delivery, I changed careers, and we moved. Despite the career and house moves, nothing changed my concept of time, space, and personal values more than the birth of my son. Moving from a two-person household to a three-person household alters you like Jello in a microwave.

The first symbol of this change was selling the sports car and buying an SUV. I am still suspicious as to whether you can change a diaper in a Mustang, but I took my wife's word for it.

Going in to this "daddy thing," I had already earned a graduate degree from Western Kentucky University in Marriage and Family Therapy. If anyone was prepared for fatherhood, surely I was. Unfortunately, "Counseling Theories" did not translate well at 2 am feedings, and "Parenting Techniques" were worthless until my son turned two. So, I had to learn some things the hard way.

Things like handling a child in a restaurant can be learned only through experience. When my son acts up, I can feel the leering eyes on me. Eyes that wonder impatiently, "When is he going to give that baby what he wants?"

I was once this naïve person, but now I am on the battleground with millions of others who can only explain, "He's a baby." I hope those without children will look on with patience as parents do their best to have a decent meal. After all, it is likely that you were once the screaming child in Cracker Barrel.

As a married couple or single person without a child, you have all these plans. In fact, according to my pre-baby time line, I should be biking over a hill in Greece right now. However, when my son was born, I learned that life was not about me, and it was not even about us (being two). Life was about "us" being three, and this can shake your family life to the ground . . . if you let it.

My dreams of selling art in Italy and of breeding dachshunds on a farm called Weiner Acres would have to wait. Why? Because I have a human who, without my wife and I, could not survive. He depends on us to supply him with everything from Goldfish crackers to proper care should he become sick (which is quite often).

The childless me wanted adventure, but now that I have a child, I see that there is no greater adventure than being with him when he sees a goose for the first time. There is no greater joy than him asking me to slide, and there is no greater warmth than seeing him hug his mama.

I am sure you feel the same about your son or daughter the human you made and who might change the world for the better. However, they can still drive you crazy.

I hope thus far some of your parenting frustrations have been alleviated. However, if you buy several new tools like a hammer or a wrench and do not have a good toolbox to put them in, you will not carry them very far. This is why I would now like to discuss general frustrations of parenting because, more than a skilled craftsman, your child needs you to be an overall good parent.

Birth Order Frustrations

For some people, parenting is just easier and birth order can play an immense part in your story as a parent. Birth order is the spot you fall in relation to your siblings and is housed within the greater context of your family of origin the home life where you were brought up.

If you are the first-born or the oldest, you may actually have a natural inclination toward parenting because you were around babies for some important developmental years. On the other hand, if you are the youngest, you will have had virtually no experience with babies. Maybe you had relatives or friends with younger children, but even then, you would naturally be repulsed by anything that looked like it would take any of the attention that you saw was rightfully yours.

Those who are the lone child in the family also have a difficult time because they have no background knowledge to pull from when rearing a child. I have an older brother and sister but basically I was raised as an only child because they were independent from Mom and Dad by the time I was five. What do I know about raising a kid? Naturally, very little, but I have had to learn so I could be a good father, and also so I could teach others.

Adapt or Die

One important aspect of surviving anything is the ability to adapt. An experienced hiker will die with a full pack of supplies all because he is in unfamiliar territory. His mind and tactic do not adjust, and that leads to his demise. Parenting is unfamiliar territory, and parents must see their children with radical acceptance to help them grow into who God wants them to be.

Do you ever feel lost as a parent? Does it seem that your idea of what should be happening with your child isn't? Maybe the path your child is taking, the level of success he is achieving, or simply his daily behavior do not quite match up with your timeline.

I struggle with this. My son is now seven, and there are times when he must know everything that Malita and I are saying. "Why must he ignore this knowledge?" I ask myself. When he was younger, I was convinced that he should be able to master a physical skill—like swinging himself on the playground, but I later discovered that some six-year-olds are unable to do that. Maybe the problem is not with him, but with me.

Not long ago, I discovered a fascinating book on wilderness survival that has given me some new insights about why parents get frustrated with their children. It has some other useful applications to my fathering. In his book *Deep Survival: Who Lives, Who Dies, and Why*, Laurence Gonzales, tells true stories of people who become lost and even die in the wilderness. He contends that people meet their ultimate demise in the wild because they fail to adapt. They apply old forms of reasoning—which he calls "mental maps"—to new experiences, and this often leads to bad decisions.

For example, even accomplished outdoorsmen sometimes struggle while hiking in unfamiliar terrain and higher altitude. They may make decisions based on past experiences, underestimate or fail to adapt to the new challenges, and miss common-sense solutions that would save them a lot of time and trouble—and maybe even their lives. They become victims because they are not willing or able to adjust their mental maps.

This mental map phenomenon is so strong. It actually caused two sailors to jump in the water with hungry sharks. Gonzalez tells the story of a boat being transported to Florida from New York. The crew got caught in a storm and lost everything but their life raft. While on the ocean for several days, the captain and first mate both slipped into the water because they thought they were getting on the deck to tie the boat down. "Pull it on up. I'll get the truck" said one of the men before getting eaten by sharks. Certainly a lack of water played a part in this tragic story, but when we do not adapt to our current situation, our minds go back to what is most familiar. The sailors did not adapt and thus were killed.

Mental maps are used in parenting as well. It could be a dad trying to relate to his daughter by applying the map of reasoning he depends on at the office. Chances are it will not work. He needs to adapt his approach to her specific needs. She is your daughter, a three or a thirteen-year-old little girl, not Phil, the jerk from accounting. Also a mom who tries to relate to her son the way she does her elementary school students will be met with little success. He is a teenager struggling with who he is, not with the temptation to eat paste.

Maybe it is more common for dads to use the faulty mental map that I call a case of the "supposed-tos." Caleb is supposed to eat what Dad tells him to. Sally is supposed to be making all A's. Timothy is supposed to be the starting quarterback. Although these may be valid expectations, our mental maps, rather than solid evidence, often drive our actions. Maybe because you were strong in a certain area, you believe your child should be too. What's wrong with this? The desire to force a child to be a certain way sacrifices the growth that could occur otherwise because it does not consider the child's unique gifts and interests.

Consequently, this inappropriate parenting impedes a lot of the good the father and mother could possibly do in shaping the child. Maybe your child is not a very gifted athlete right now. He may never be if he feels pressure to perform beyond his capabilities. This is a faulty mental map that has not adapted. Forcing a child to perform is like training for a sport by skipping the basics.

A measure of dysfunction in a family is the inability to adapt. If you do not adapt to your child becoming a five-year-old, you may continue to treat him like an infant. If you do not accept the fact that your child is now driving, he may never learn an adequate amount of independence.

All too often parents use mental maps such as I described with my son. We assume we know how quickly our children should be progressing in life, and we try to force our own time line on them, overlooking their talents and developmental growth. It took me three years to reach my weight-lifting goal. Had I been forced into a shorter time line, I may have never attained it and possibly could have been seriously injured. Your daughter can possibly be the best softball player in town, but if her spirit is wrecked from ridicule because she is not making immense strides, you can forget it. Little by little, children can excel, and we must respect that. That's not me talking; it's nature.

What's a better approach? I have two suggestions:

First, check your motivation for why you are pushing your son or daughter to succeed. Is it for his good or for your own? There is a deep pride that fathers carry when their children succeed at something. When you see a glimmer of talent in a child, excitement takes over, and it may take over so much that your child's acceleration to the next skill level may be impaired because of your desire to get him or her there too quickly. It's important to distinguish between your own dreams and desires for your child and what is truly best for him.

Now, if your encouragement and prodding are based on evidence of the child's talents and past accomplishments, then that may be a different matter. Children can be lazy unless they are pushed to do their best, but please make sure they can reach the goals you set for them. If your goals are too lofty, your child could fail repeatedly and become discouraged.

Second, you must understand your child. Ask yourself, "What is he good at and how can I help him get better?" Focus on discovering a child's strengths and then helping him capitalize on those strengths. Avoid comparing him to other kids or basing your expectations on some other faulty mental map of where you think he should be. By stepping back and analyzing the situation, you can get a clearer grasp of where your child is, which will greatly increase the chances that your actions as a father will help him achieve his full potential. You may need to give up on some of your own goals and expectations for your child, but it's much better for the child in the end.

Dad, if you're like me, you are often very quick—sometimes too quick—to jump in and fix things. If my first attempt doesn't work, I sometimes get frustrated and do more damage than what was there at the start. (We're more emotional than we'd like to admit sometimes.) Please do take action to help your child follow his dreams and find success in life, but please take it slowly. Sometimes, as hard as it is, you just need to stop and think. When you understand your child and what he needs from you, you're much better prepared. That's the best mental map for your fatherhood. Another great benefit of understanding your child is that it will naturally lead to a tighter bond with him or her.

Anger as a Tool?

We may have it laid out in our mental maps what we hope our children to become, but what about day-to-day stuff? How can we find joy in this and be less frustrated "where the rubber meets the road?" We can have good times with our kids at ballgames, birthday parties, and at church events. But unless we can reach our children while sitting on their beds or while driving in the car alone, we may not reach them. We must be able to mold our children at all times because, even when we are not around, we want our words to permeate their thoughts and actions.

What do you feel most often when your kids misbehave or act "unbecomingly?" You probably feel anger, and a lot of the times it is justified. However, anger and frustration are difficult to bear. I am sure most parents would like to relinquish as much of this burden as possible. One way is to use better parenting strategies and allow them to do their job. Another method is based on your relationship with anger. Some parents love anger and believe it to be a good molding tool for their children. If you are angry, say so. Just do not let yourself be a rage-aholic. Your child needs guidance from a level-headed adult.

When you are angry, you are wishing things were different than what they are. You can be angry with our children, yes, but I believe you are angry much more often than you need to be. Because you want things to be different with your child, you become angry, but remember, he is a child or a teen. He is constantly going to break things, disobey you, and run amuck of your life and house. Accept this and work with it. What do they gain if they make you mad? Not a lot. They are miserable. Do you remember your teen years?

You were probably miserable too, but you wanted someone to help make the misery stop. If just one adult knew how to talk to you, you would feel so much better. If only one knew exactly what to say, you would have been able to sleep better. Be the guide your child needs. She is lost in her world, and she is angry about it. Do not let your anger cloud your decisions as you work to bring her out of the abyss.

Some Joy Is Already There

I write for a parenting blog titled EmpoweringParents.com. On it parents talk a lot about their child who misbehaves, and why shouldn't they? Have you ever seen a website devoted to getting help with your well-behaved child? Probably not, but a well-behaved child is often an overlooked child, particularly if there are siblings who act out and take most of the parents' attention. Here are some things to keep in mind when you have a child who is a proverbial "good" kid:

First, give them attention. Just because your child behaves well does not mean they don't need attention. The "bad" kid in your family usually monopolizes this resource because he requires so much of it to keep him in line. But remember that your well-behaved child wants to do things, and he wants to do them with you. Even if he can play video games, watch TV and read all day long without the slightest redirection from you, the things that will really help him excel are what he does with you. Don't forget him. Particularly as he gets older, he needs you to be in his life. Some parents think it should be less, but this is simply not true. Make time to do things your child likes and learn to enjoy them. The time spent together is the most important thing.

Second, be careful not to turn your good kid into a bad one. Understand that your child will mess up sometimes, but it's not the end of the world. Sometimes parent/child stress can come from a parent who thinks their son or daughter should not ever do anything wrong. This expectation level can drive a child to high anxiety, depression, or even suicide.

Finally, be thankful for what your kids are, not for what they are not. I was visiting a hospital one evening with my family. My son was running and my daughter was being loud. Thankfully we were in a part of the hospital with no patients. A doctor passed me and said I was the luckiest man he'd seen that day. He was right. We were in a public place and my kids were being rambunctious, but so what? No one was being disturbed and they were having fun. What if my boy couldn't run or what if my girl couldn't yell? Kids are going to be kids. Parents must learn to accept this, reprimand when necessary and enjoy when appropriate.

Joy With a Misbehaving Child?

Finding the joy is difficult because you are often still reeling from the last three things your rambunctious child or ungrateful teen did. Sometimes I feel that all I ever tell my little girl is, "Stop! You'll get hurt." This sense of frustration can be particularly true with teens especially who have learned to manipulate and really push your buttons. How can you possibly find joy in something that seems bent on getting the best of you? Remember, you are trying to guide them. They do not know (either by lack of knowledge or development) exactly how they are affecting you, but you know how you can and must affect them. It can be difficult to come down from the emotional roller coaster your child puts you on. Anger, frustration, and disappointment are difficult to handle. However, it is possible in the midst of chaos to join with your children and enjoy them.

The middle schoolers I work with are notorious for blaming their actions on something or someone else. "My mom didn't tell me to do my homework." " I can't help it when I yell." These are just a few of the excuses teachers hear regularly. I try to teach students that we are responsible for our actions; we choose them. Given the go-ahead, some middle schoolers would smack every person that ever made them mad. "I don't like what you said, so I can do this. I can't help it." We must teach our children a better way because the impulsive reactions we have to slap every person who upsets us must be overcome.

Most adults get a hold on their emotions with great success. They are not as wildly emotional as they were when they were teens. But what about when it comes to your child? When she back talks you, does a screaming match ensue? When you have told him ten times to clean his room, do you just do it yourself? These actions can certainly suck the joy out of parenting and really make you not like your beloved offspring. However, if you choose joy, you can truly enjoy your child again.

First, follow the principles in this book. By utilizing the tools here, and in other parenting resources, you can feel better knowing that you are parenting with a purpose. You have boundaries, consequences, and a sense that by employing solid parenting tactics you are making better parenting decisions. Therefore, you will lose some of the guilt associated with thinking you have somehow made a mistake.

Second, talk to other parents and your spouse about your frustrations. Nothing can make you so lonely as believing you are alone in a battle. When you discuss how you handled certain situations, other adults who have had success can validate you. Sharing the burden makes it easier to bear.

Third, when the punishment is done, let it be done. Ask yourself, "Do I want to be angry for the rest of the evening?" "No." This is the critical point when you choose not to be angry any more. Take some time away from your child and let yourself cool down, but do not let it ruin what could be made into a good night.

Finally, make something happen. What do you and your child like to do together? End the night on a good note. Read or watch a movie together because the final experience is the lasting experience. By going to bed on good terms with one another, you will rest better and start the day basically where you left off; amiable.

Conclusion

The frustrations we experience as parents can be overwhelming. We pour our everything into something we care deeply about only to be met with resistance. The heartache is equally as devastating. We must keep in mind that the seeds we plant may not grow until much later. Our returns are not a 1:1 ratio, but if we accept the game that we are in and work to play by rules that we have a great deal of control over, we can come out victorious in the end.

Questions for Discussion

1. How do you cope with the frustrations of parenting?

2. What can you handle better this week that you have been struggling with?

3. What are you coping better with now that was once a struggle for you?

CHAPTER 11

Understanding Your Child's Behavior and Misbehavior

I hear both parents and teachers comment on how their children act. Frustrated, they will say, "Why can't you act like a sixth grader?" or "Why can't you act like a ten-year-old?" The funny thing is, they probably are.

Children and teens throw things, burp, and talk when they are not supposed to simply because they are kids. Let us not forget that as adults we are raising children who do not always know how to act and who often love doing what they are not supposed to. This may seem oversimplified, but many adults need to remember this. It can really take away the unending burden of wanting a child always to act a certain way. Let him be a child and know when to correct and know when to let him run, jump, and scream.

I have spoken with frustrated parents about what they needed to do to turn their child's behavior around, and typically all that is needed is for them to understand the motivation behind the behavior. This will help them counteract and even accept their child for the imperfect being that he is.

All people act in ways that make sense to them. I did not say that the behavior made sense. It simply makes sense to the person behaving (or not behaving).

Your Child's Behavior

Nature vs. Nurture

We have already discussed family systems theory. So it should be evident that your child's behavior is a direct response to what you are doing (or not doing) to, with, and for him. This is the nurture side of the nature vs. nurture argument in psychoanalysis. Nature vs. nurture begs the question, "How much of a person's actions come from how they were raised versus the traits they are born with?" Why do identical twins, separated at birth, have so much in common? Certainly, your child's inherent personality, which some believe is developed as early as age two, plays a part in their behavior. But just as you can steer a Ferrari down the highway, you can also steer a pick-up truck. It is just a matter of knowing how.

What types of behavior are you feeding? Narcissism? Entitlement? Autonomy? Inferiority? How a child acts reflects how she feels about herself and about the world around him. Certainly, she is a cute little girl and the apple of her daddy's eyes. But if she is rude to the ladies at church and believes that she can get whatever she wants, then do not be surprised when she acts like this toward you. If misbehavior is not recognized and corrected, it will continue.

Some parents try to explain the behavior away. In his book, *Systematic Training for Effective Teaching* (STET), Dr. Don Dinkmeyer explains popular, but not very helpful, theories about why kids act the way they do.

Dad hollered like that. This blames heredity (nature) and gives the child a free pass to act the way he wants. Self-control is neglected.

It's not us. It's everything around us. This blames the environment (nurture). Parents move into a better neighborhood to go to a better school and have more patient teachers, but Tommy's behavior does not change. In fact, it gets worse, but why does his little sister still act so good?

It's just a stage (nature). "Oh, he'll grow out of this." True to an extent. Ask a child to look at the moon and ask her if it follows her, she will say "yes." Children have no concept of the world outside what they see in front of them. This is developmentally appropriate. But if you wait for your child to "grow out of it" are you allowing father time to parent your child, or are you going to help shape his thinking. Left uncorrected and unchallenged, a child's behavior will worsen to fit the child's needs.

Boys will be boys and girls will be girls (nature and nurture). Wow! I heard a story on the news once about two teens who raped a girl. One of the boy's fathers went to the justice and said, "Boys will be boys." God gave us the Ten Commandments so we could learn right from wrong. Excuse a child's behavior because they are "supposed" to do it and the behavior will continue.

All children are like this (nature). Parents are notorious for comparing their child to others. We want to make sure he is growing and developing correctly so some comparison is healthy. Otherwise, you would not really know what is and is not normal. However, what we expect often comes true. Do you expect bad behavior?

Are *You* Misbehaving?

Parents get a lot of pride from giving their children what they need. For some, it is the ability to give their children what they never had. My father grew up in a log cabin and woke up during the winter months with frost on the five quilts that were keeping him warm. Don't you think he felt pride, being able to install an HVAC unit in our home, helping us to live like kings, comparatively.

My mother took me to football practice and anywhere else I needed to go after school to feed what she thought would help me. She fed the good in me and watched it grow. Sure, I watched TV after school, but only after practice and my homework was done.

Parents also get a lot of self-satisfaction when giving their children what they want. To supply a child with his needs is one thing, but to live in such a way that your child can have more, that he can have beyond what you dreamed of as a child, makes a parent feel good. He is the one with the latest toy. He is the one with the coolest birthday party for the year. He is the one who has all the right clothes.

Do not get your parental satisfaction from material things. You can be the cool parent and provide more than what he needs, but this must be balanced. Is there a genuine appreciation from your child? Does he think of others before himself? These questions will help you see if your child's behavior is headed in the right direction. If at your birthday party he acts like a tyrant, you correct him, and he does not express the least bit of remorse, it is time to change your game plan.

Too many parents have not the foggiest idea that this is how things should be done. They allow their child to do what he wants to do because he wants to do it. Given the opportunity, any child will choose the easy path of fun. That path does not make one grow into a Christian, but rather one that thinks only of oneself.

Your Child's Misbehavior

Dr. Dinkmeyer's work was originally for parents. His book *Systematic Training for Effective Parenting* (STEP) was first published in the 1980s and is still an effective parenting tool today. In STEP, Dr. Dinkmeyer discusses the four short-term goals of misbehavior first observed by Rudolf Dreikurs. Children misbehave because:

1. They want *attention*.
2. They want *power*.
3. They are looking for *revenge*.
4. They have given up, want you to leave them alone, and thereby choose to *display their inadequacy*.

When you understand your child's goals for misbehavior, you can redirect your child in a more positive direction. You can remove the emotional side of your reaction which often thwarts anything positive the parent could actually do. This will involve changing your behavior to changing theirs because their actions are a direct response to you.

How can you tell which of these four your child is utilizing? First, look at yourself. How do you feel when your child misbehaves? If you are annoyed, the behavior is probably for attention. If you are angry, the behavior was for power as your authority has been challenged. If you were hurt, his actions were out of revenge, and if you feel sad for your child, his actions were likely because he feels inadequate over something.

Remember; do not look at the behavior itself. "Why won't you do your homework? Why won't you clean your room? Why can't I get you to act right?" The specific actions need to be handled, but only after you have pinpointed the motivation. Otherwise, your response will fall on deaf ears because you are not getting to the heart of the matter.

Second, Dr. Dinkmeyer suggests that you consider how the child responds when reprimanded. Did he stop making that noise, but just for a second, and then start again? This helps him get attention. Did he ignore you when you asked him to turn off the TV? He is exercising his power and is saying, "I'll do it when I want." Did he look at you menacingly? Will he find a way to get back at you? Did he start crying and call himself names like "stupid?" He wants to play the victim so you will ease up on him.

Attention

Babies learn to get our attention very early. They figure out that when they cry, something happens. He gets changed, he gets fed, he gets picked up. Crying is our very first method for controlling the world around us, and we like it.

It is also a necessary method because babies cannot do anything else.

Most all children and teens enjoy attention. Come work with me for a day and observe all the ways middle schoolers compete for attention from their peers and from their teachers. Good or bad, it does not matter, students crave the attention they get, and they often work to get more and more. There is a natural inclination by children to get people to notice them, but are there other reasons?

When a child or a teen craves attention, it is often because they are not getting it from the normal sources. Because his family may be dysfunctional or even non-existent, the child will seek a family unit through gangs or just friends at school. He will act up in class because that is the only way he knows to get attention from the matriarchal figure in the room, his teacher. He is starving and is getting what he needs the only way he knows how. Furthermore, the child may not be particularly bright, but his/her sibling is good at everything. This child gets pushed to the side because Mom and Dad spend so much time with the "Hero" of the family. The misfit cannot do anything good, so he does bad things.

The child learns that the only way he can get attention is by being annoying. This is easy to do. Tap your fork on the table, tap your pencil on your desk, or my favorite is a really big yawn in the middle of my in-class lecture. All attention is now on the child.

Why is your child lacking attention? I have found that they will want your every waking moment if you give it to them, but we do have to go to work. This craving for your constant companionship can be a sign of a lack of independence or self-reliance—an inability to engage in self-directed play and a constant dependence on the parents in the home. On the other hand, if your child is dependent, but is constantly acting out, how much positive time do you spend with him? You may say that there is no time because he is always acting poorly. This may be the case, but positive behavior needs to be noticed. Even if you simply notice an absence of outright hostility, you can find ways to give positive attention to the child. Hopefully, he will enjoy the positive and begin to move toward that behavior more.

Power

People enjoy being in control of their environment. We all like our space on the pew at church and on the couch at home. We like what we call "our stuff," and we do not want people to bother it. Some children however have the personality that compels them to be in control more than the average child. He or she takes charge at playtime and is indignant when people do not listen to his commands. This behavior is often encouraged in the toddler years, "Yes. She is little miss bossy-pants." Certainly, a take-charge attitude can and should be a positive thing. Much like the attention-seeking child, they can use their lack of inhibition to thrive; the natural tendency for your child to lead can be used for good too. However, if you are at odds with your child because of this desire to control, you must figure out a way to reach him. Otherwise, you will continually be in a power struggle, totally squashing your ability to influence your child for good.

When a power struggle begins, you are typically angered. Your child has ignored your command and your authority has been challenged. What should you do? First, this dynamic should stop even before it gets started. Assume that your child is going to do what you ask and press upon him this fact. You do not expect to ask him two more times. You do expect him to comply immediately or within a reasonable amount of time. If he needs to take the trash out, be flexible and allow him to finish his game, ask him to pause it or wait until a commercial. Is it really important that it be done right then? If you told him an hour ago to do it and it still is not done, then yes. He should not be relaxing when there is work to be done. However, if you just noticed it and he has not, do you really want to start a power struggle where one does not have to be? Plus, admit it, you would wait until a commercial too. To avoid this, you can also set a guideline that after dinner he is to take out the trash or after school he is to walk the dog. This will serve as a healthy reminder and give him a way to remember.

Second, give them the power they want so badly when it is appropriate. Henry Ford said of the Model T that the consumer could have any color he wanted so long as it was black. Your son can have any curfew he wants so long as it's between 10 and 11 pm. Your daughter can go to bed with any doll she wants. If you will notice, the act that you want done is not in question, but you have given them appropriate options. She can talk on her phone whenever she wants but only after her chores are done. It is their choice (power) to do whatever they want, but you are setting parameters.

Revenge

This sounds malicious and like a behavior that only the most deviant of children would utilize, but it is actually a more prominent behavior than you think. Think of it as a back-up plan for when power fails. Your child may not win the power struggle but she can make you and everyone else miserable when she does not get her way. Think of a child who would proclaim a hunger strike when he or she did not get to choose the restaurant. "Since we are not going to eat where I want, I just won't eat." Some parents would jump to try and get the child to eat, but eating is one thing we cannot make children do. It is a legitimate power they have. We can only give them choices. "Eat this or that. Eat this or nothing." When the child says she won't eat, this is her way of making you feel sympathy for her.

This revenge tactic can stem from when their power fails. Imagine your child is arguing with you over something and you finally get your point across. The child will then work to make you miserable somehow. Because she cannot go out with her friends, she is going to make everyone's evening at home as unpleasant as possible. Most children and teens do not methodically plot this way; it is simply what is happening.

To counteract this, allow the consequences of the child's actions to take effect. If she has to stay home that weekend, she can still be involved in your family's activities. If your child decides she is not going to eat, she can still have whatever she wants on the menu. By doing this you do not take out your own revenge on the child.

Poor Me

Everyone likes to be catered to, but some make a career of it, working their way in the hearts of the parents to have everything done for them. "I can't find the answer to number two, can you help me?" Because every parent hates to see their child in distress, they will run to their aid. "Look, it's in this paragraph." Homework is done quicker, but the student is not learning about perseverance. What he/she has learned is that if they act pitiful enough, long enough, they will have an easier time. However, Mom and Dad are not doing their child any good by aiding in their pity parties.

"It's too difficult" or "I'm so stupid" are also common cries of a child who pulls on his parents' heartstrings. An effective way to teach swimming is to put the child in the water. You cannot teach swimming on land. Eventually, you have to get wet. Then, eventually, you have to let your child go to do it all by himself. Never do for your child what he can do himself.

Correcting Behavior

While walking through a local mall, I saw a mother give her six-year-old daughter a firm swat on her posterior. She followed this reprimand with, "Don't you ever hit me." This is ironic because she hit her for hitting, but I do not fault Mom for what she did. In fact, I understand wanting to let my son know immediately that what he did was wrong and spanking is often a good choice. It seemed like the best one then since there are no "time out" chairs next to Sbarro's.

The messages we send our children need to be loud and clear and a smack on the bottom does this. It is the one thing you can do to your child that he cannot really do to you effectively. Furthermore, parents do not have to give an explanation for their decisions, and "because I said so" is good enough. However, raising a child with these sentiments will be frustratingly slow because what your mama did in the 1980s is not going to work too well these days. Correcting your child's behavior should open a door to affect them, and by not helping them understand the reason for your administered consequences, you choose to keep them in the dark on something you really want them to understand.

Now, I am the first in line when a child needs to be spanked. I just believe there are some good alternatives to spanking that your son or daughter will understand more and even appreciate as they learn valuable lessons. To ensure that your child is learning something every time you correct them, some creativity and common sense must be utilized. This will, in the long run, make it easier on both of you.

There are two types of consequences that curb bad behavior: logical and natural. Natural consequences happen as the result of a child's actions. Maybe you told him not to leave his bike in the driveway because it might get run over. Not knowing that it is there, you back out of the garage and destroy his prized possession. This is a natural consequence that will teach many lessons as he works to buy a new one.

Logical consequences are what you set forth as consequences for your child's actions. This might be time-outs or the removal of privileges. The child does x and the result is y. I do not believe extra chores are good punishments because children should be doing extra chores anyway. Plus, you want them to equate work with a good feeling, not something negative. It is important too that the consequence go hand-in-hand with the offense.

Making her wash dishes because she was late for curfew hardly teaches a lesson. However, not going out for the next two weeks is specifically tied to what she did wrong.

Children love surprises, but not when it comes to punishment. Do not enforce anything you have not clearly spoken to your child about. Natural consequences must be allowed to flow because hey, "that's life," and logical consequences should be a regular part of your family dynamic. You use them regularly, and your child associates his/her behavior with the outcome of a punishment. This is how you can guide your child even when you are not around.

Framing this appropriately will help your child learn and take some of the pressure off of you. Think of it this way. You are not punishing her, but rather she chose the punishment when she broke the rule. As she tries to argue with you in the hopes that the punishment will be revoked, just keep reminding her that it is not your problem, but that she chose to be grounded next week when she chose to break curfew. It was her decision, not yours.

What About Spanking?

Spanking is good because it is swift and effective. Scripture teaches us much and here is no exception. "He who withholds his rod hates his son, but he who loves him disciplines him diligently" (Proverbs 13:24). There were few child psychologists in biblical times, so the idea of not spanking your child would be quite foreign to the people of the day. This verse mentions the rod, but it also mentions love. A parent who loves and disciplines with a rod would not do so to the degree of abuse, but simply to get the point across. I would also venture to say that with the standard of punishment being so severe, there were few child behavior problems then. Certainly nothing like we have today.

"Foolishness is bound up in the heart of a child; the rod of discipline will remove it far from him" (Proverbs 22:15). I love these passages. Not because I enjoy beating my child, but because I have seen it work first-hand. Children do not know how to reason. They do not understand how their behavior now will affect them in the future, but they do understand a swift belt. If you have tried all the passive tactics, maybe it is time to try something that everyone can grasp. As the old saying goes, "Spare the rod and spoil the child." If you do not follow this saying, you will completely change its syntax to, "Spare the rod, AND spoil the child."

According to Canadian researchers in an article in a 2012 issue of

Pediatrics, children who are spanked are more likely to have a mental illness as adults. These mental illnesses include depression, anxiety, alcohol and drug abuse as well as personality disorders that may be attributable to physical punishment. Physical punishment was defined as pushing, grabbing, shoving, slapping. More severe maltreatment of a child through physical abuse, sexual abuse, emotional abuse, physical neglect, emotional neglect or spousal abuse was not included.

I find anti-spanking studies like this one to be too broad, and they often, by their design and proclamation, mislead people. You can say anything you want with statistics. It is broad in that they lump spanking with "slapping, pushing, hitting, grabbing and shoving." My goodness. I would never do those and one can certainly imagine how repeated slapping across the face could scar someone emotionally. Something is very offensive about that form of "punishment." When a person slaps another on the face, it is to disregard the portion of our physical body wherewith we join in love through speech and kissing. Our posteriors, on the other hand, seem to be engineered for the purpose of correction.

I do spank, although rarely. Too much needs to be taught through things like natural and logical consequences and positive reinforcement in which I truly believe. However, sometimes talking and positive reinforcement will not work when the child is smart enough to work the system. "Give me a reward and I'll do what you ask." OR "Counting to five before you do something, mom? OK, I have four more seconds to disobey." If this is the case, you have a real problem on your hands.

It seems that in these studies, everyone targets spanking, but sometimes they fail to mention the other forms of violence defined. Shoving a seven year old to the floor for spilling milk should not be equated with my swatting my two-year-old's leg for disobeying or not listening. Spankings get attention when other tactics fail.

In homes where spanking is the only form of discipline, probably a lot more behaviors (other than spanking) are to be found that would lead to the mentioned disorders. A disregard for a child's comprehensive emotional development can easily be equated with a parent who shoves, grabs and hits. It can be said that parents who raise children into adults with the aforementioned problems do spank. It is not necessarily true that "spanking causes these problems," although this conclusion is often derived from people who read such studies; therefore it is misleading. Tracie Afifi, author of the study, acknowledged, "It's not a causal effect and the study design can't prove the link," but she said, "The statistical association is clear." Association is much different than causality. It seems that every time I go camping, it rains. So, there is an association, but the fact that I am camping did not cause the rain.

I think spanking often gets used too quickly. It should never be used when you are out of control and angry. I am just not willing to say that it should never be used especially when it is equated in a study with shoving and slapping. Finally, I am a firm believer in God's wisdom, more so than man's. "He who withholds his rod hates his son, but he who loves him disciplines him diligently" (Proverbs 13:24).

Five Rules About Spanking

1. **Ask yourself, "Do I need to teach my child a lesson?"** Spanking only teaches "no" and this is necessary, but if you could teach a child more, why wouldn't you? This is where the logical and natural consequences come in handy.

2. **Ask yourself, "Am I angry?"** You should never spank your child when you are angry or out of control. Think of the image from your child's point of view. Quite scary. You are not thinking clearly and again, point number one may be forgotten.

3. **Only spank on your child's bottom or swat the leg quickly.** The backside is sufficiently padded to absorb shock and a child's leg is quick to get to and effective with just one slap. This is useful for young children who have the inability to reason. I want my child to learn now, not when she has had three to four years to gain cognitive ability and learn how to work the system.

4. **Does your child understand that what he did was wrong?** Does your two-year-old know that sticking her tongue out is wrong? When you tell her to stop and she doesn't, then swatting her leg helps her associate her behavior with a negative experience.

5. **Don't hit too hard.** If coupled with a child who does not want to disappoint you, swatting hard will not be necessary. The humiliation of getting spanked is enough for some children. If your child laughs at you, try something else.

Conclusion

Raising children is like handling a butterfly, you must do what you can to keep the delicate creature in your grasp without crushing it. So, we must give careful consideration to the way we redirect the behavior of our children; otherwise, we might send mixed or unclear messages that do not effectively get the point across.

Questions for Discussion

1. What in your home influences your child's behavior?

2. What is your child's primary reason for misbehavior?

3. What are your top three ways to discipline your child?

CHAPTER 12

Discipline Is Necessary.
It's Good for Children Too

I have spoken with frustrated parents about what they needed to do to turn around their child's behavior. They will tell me what is going on; I will work to understand it and then suggest some interventions. However, all too often, it is like I am speaking a different language. I explain multiple, well-proven tactics for parenting, and the response I have received is, "Well, if you can think of anything that I can do, let me know."

There is an unspoken rule that some parents believe, "My child is misbehaving so something must be wrong with *him*." More often than not, the child is fine. Children do silly things, act up at inappropriate times, and even talk back. If they did otherwise, they would not need parents. It is always surprising to me when parents say, "Why do you act that way?" I often want to say, "Because he is a child." The following has been said of our youth:

> "Our youth now love luxury. They have bad manners, contempt for authority; they show disrespect for their elders and love chatter in place of exercise; they no longer rise when elders enter the room; they contradict their parents, chatter before company; gobble up their food, and tyrannize their teachers."

This quotation is attributed to Socrates well over two thousand years ago. Youth has changed some, but not really. They are exactly the same in many ways. It is the parents who are different because they are new at parenting. They are new at being adults. A child is excellent at being a child. It is the parent who must work to shape and mold the child.

For a parent to instill discipline, respect, and all sorts of other character traits in a child, the parent must have self-discipline, live a life of self-examination, and be willing to do whatever it takes to raise that child. This includes seeing your child for what he or she is; a being who succumbs to the push and pull of their emotions, basic desires, and uninformed intellect. You must see what is going on with your child. Is he controlling you? Are you letting the world raise him or her? Do you have the courage to stand up and be the parent they need?

Is Your Child Controlling You?

Everyone likes to be in control of things, and children are no exception. They learn early on that if they cry, they'll be fed or changed. This behavior has its purpose, and the goal of parents is to help their child become more co-operative over time. Sadly, many children don't learn this and go on to train their parents quite effectively. From crying to arguing, your child may be controlling you.

First, do you find yourself regularly defending misbehavior? A teacher sends home a note citing specific misdeeds. You ask what happened, and your son states he didn't understand the rule. You then write a poignant letter describing why your beloved prince acted the way he did. Your child has learned to escape consequences by making excuses and soliciting your help. If this continues, he will never learn to control his actions. No amount of defiance, deficit, or "I didn't know" should ever be good enough to excuse poor behavior.

Secondly, do you argue with your child a lot? A child who argues regularly knows that if she can wear you down, she'll get her way. Furthermore, if she doesn't get her way, she'll make you angry and miserable in the process. Even if you win, you lose. You're the parent. Listen to your child, make a decision, and stick to it. No debating. Otherwise, you will be clamoring for a decision, wondering what the argument was all about in the first place.

Third, are arguments between you and your spouse often caused by your child? The big word for this is triangulation, but it's also called "Divide and Conquer." Son speaks to parent A, who says "no," so he goes to parent B acting like a victim. Parent B defends the child making parent A, look bad. Mom and Dad must be cohorts in child-rearing, not enemies.

Fourth, do you go to great lengths to keep her happy? Your child is just that, a child. She is not really a princess. She should be made to wait, share, and cooperate. Being uncomfortable teaches a child that the world does not revolve around her. This is how you can effectively teach the concept of servanthood to your child (Matthew 20:16). She must learn that the greatest satisfaction comes from helping others, not in getting her way.

In all of the above examples the child is working to get what he or she *wants*. Parents must be in the business of giving their children what they *need*. If you agree with me, then you are probably right on track in parenting. However, if you became defensive, maybe you should begin taking back the power that is rightfully yours.

We must learn children's tactics of control; otherwise they will use them to get out of one of their best learning experiences: consequences.

Let Children Learn on Their Own

In 2007, at Discovery Canyon Campus school in Denver, CO, assistant principal, Cindy Fesgen banned the game of tag because it caused a lot of conflict on the playground. "Children complained they were harassed or chased against their will." My wife and I both work in the school system, and sometimes it is necessary to stop children from being too rough. However, I can imagine that what probably happened was a parent, known for starting trouble, complained to the administration, who then clicked their heels and said, "Yes, ma'am." They were not thinking about what was best for the entire student body, but only about oiling the squeaky wheel. Athletic games have not been totally taken away, but spontaneous "just for fun" chases have been pushed aside. I'm sure that kickball will be the next victim. [1]

Are we raising a spineless generation? Are we raising a generation that will be dependent on its parents through adulthood? We'll definitely need more therapists because young people are not taught vital character traits like self-reliance and perseverance. You do not want your child to get hurt, but you also do not want him living in your basement when he is thirty-five; a real issue in today's world.

Conflict is a part of life, and if students do not experience it, they will not learn to handle it. This is why parents should be about training children to be self-reliant. How can a child's faith be "tried by fire" if he/she is not allowed to be at least a little uncomfortable?

Sometimes the best way to do this is to allow things to happen. One night at my son's soccer game, I watched as two brothers fought over a toy. The little one had thrown it so the older boy took it back. After the smaller one shed a few tears, big brother asked him not to throw it again and then returned the item. Mom and Dad were standing right there, but they allowed the boys to work it out.

Should an adult intervene for children? Most certainly, but only to help them deal with things constructively. While not the school's intent in Colorado, they allowed reverse bullying to take place. "I can't play your game, so you can't play it at all." There were countless alternatives besides outlawing the game.

In the third grade I jumped off the monkey bars and landed on a girl, severely breaking her leg in two places. It was an accident, no one was sued, and we remained friends as well as next-door neighbors for many more years. If this happened today, some schools might remove every piece of equipment taller than three feet or tether students to whatever they wanted to play on.

When the prodigal son asked his father for his inheritance, the father did not protest. He gave his son what he had coming to him and allowed him to leave. Through the subsequent experience the son realized, "My dad is really smart, and he knows what he is talking about." Most teens learn as they get older that their parents are pretty wise.

I wonder how much parents in similar situations have gone through to get to the point of allowing their child to experience the dangers of this world? How much have parents heard, "I hate living here! I want out!!" How much turmoil have these parents been through to show they have their teen's best interest in mind? They have tried to lead and guide, but the realization finally occurs that says, "I've got to let them learn the hard way."

God, being the creator of mankind, also loses children. I love what Psalm 81 says in verses 11-13 "But My people did not listen to My voice, and Israel did not obey Me. So I gave them over to the stubbornness of their heart, to walk in their own devices. Oh that My people would listen to Me, that Israel would walk in My ways!" A beautiful passage that illustrates what our Father in heaven has done and what parents on earth must do: allow our children to learn on their own through experience. For your five-year-old it might be perseverance that he learns through the trial of riding on his bike. For your fifteen-year-old daughter it might be that she learns to trust your judgment after having her heart broken. This learning involves a separation, but exactly how large should this separation be?

How Wide Should the Divide Be?

Although you are making sure that your child isn't running the show and that he/she is actually learning things through experience, be sure not to get too far away from them. Our local high school was told by its board of education to pull the book, *Looking for Alaska* by John Green from an English class because of a detailed description of sex between two teens. Obviously, this is inappropriate. There was a slight uproar on both sides of this issue, but in the end, the board made the right decision. People complained and letters were sent, but thankfully decency won.

What bothers me more about this entire issue is actually hidden from plain sight. What is hidden is the belief that kids can decide for themselves what they want to read.

When a person says, "Teens should be allowed to read the book," they are assuming that the teen has the final say over what he/she does. This is what is wrong with adults today. Adults believe that a teen can find her own way. That she can take care of herself. I've seen too many girls destroy themselves to believe this is good parenting. I've seen too many girls who needed to be dragged out of their drug dealer's house to think that a teen or, for that matter, a good-intentioned adult can take care of my child better than I can. Whether it's in relationships, personal behavior, or even literature, a teen should not have the final say in what he does. If he did, parents wouldn't be needed.

Parents are guides; parents are to be mentors; and parents are to screen things that come into their children's lives. All too often, parents reach out and grasp at air when trying to stop their teen from destructive behavior. They have waited too long and have allowed a gulf to separate them. By the late teen years, the expanse is so great that the parent has little to no influence over the child.

There will be struggles, rebellion, and lots of rolled eyes from the teen, but it is our job to lead them and help them take on values that we believe will get them through life. It's my child, not the school's. If this means skipping a book, so be it. There are plenty more to read.

What Can You Do?

Parenting is a difficult job because so many things are vying for our children. Products are peddled to younger generations in the hopes that the items will be purchased. Future customers? Right! Politicians and special interest groups may try to sway younger generations in ways that are counter to your values. If the young people can be changed, more things will be accepted in the future things that may go against your Christian worldview. Some people work at enabling your child's bad behavior. Whether it's an influential adult, friend, or even doctor, you need to be on the lookout for anything that might keep you from doing your job appropriately as a parent.[2]

You must take an active role in your child's life. By allowing them to read what they want, watch what they want, and be influenced heavily by this world, you are taking a risk. It may be more than a risk as you send them to the wolves of this world. Our society no longer prizes devotion to God, but rather doing what one feels is right. There is no thought of Scripture; rather only a pandering to the masses of political correctness.

Teach your child to determine right and wrong. Proverbs 14:7 says, "Leave the presence of a fool or you will not discern words of knowledge." In our world, there are no absolutes because I am right and you are right. There cannot be two opposing correct answers to something. You must arm your child for the fight of faith. Do not allow them to go out into this world among wolves without having a strong foundation. Discuss the news and the day's events, and then what is right or wrong about them in the eyes of God. You do not do this to promote a political agenda or to shape your child for a future occupation. Rather, you do this to raise a Christian who can go out on his own and be a champion for Christ.

Be aware of your school's policies on things like sex education. Although most do an excellent job of educating students, they can do a lousy job of giving to a child exactly what she needs. They work to educate the masses, and within those masses are students who need sex education. But as a Christian parent, you have a deep desire for your child to get very specific messages about character and decency.

Finally, be strong for your child. Know what is going on in his life. He deserves privacy, trust, and respect, but only if he earns it.

Questions for Discussion

1. How have children changed and not changed since your age of development?

2. At what age should children be made to do what chores?

3. What boundaries do you have for your children in regard to things that you believe are harmful?

Notes

1. Springs principal bans kids' game Article 1 of 1 found

   Kieran Nicholson

   Denver Post Staff Writer

   August 31, 2007; Page B-01

   Section: DENVER AND WEST

   Article ID: 1374401—430 words

   Colorado Springs—"Tag, you're it!" The seemingly eternal phrase that kids squeal on playgrounds and in schoolyards across the country won't be heard at an elementary school in Colorado Springs.

   The pre-K through fifth-grade school at Discovery Canyon Campus, a Colorado Springs District 20 school, has banned tag on its playground.

   "Students will not be playing Click for complete article ($2.95)

2. http://www.advocatesforyouth.org/index.php?option=com_content&task=view&id=516&Itemid=336

CHAPTER 13

Our Heavenly Father Is a Parent

While at a youth day in Bowling Green, KY, in 2004, a young man stood before us and spoke of his two children. I was at least three or four years older than this guy and he already had two children? I felt behind, but more importantly I felt like I needed to do something. It was time for Malita and me to have our first child.

By this time I had been working with young people in some youth ministry capacity since I was seventeen. I was twenty-seven at the time and I knew that I loved kids. However, nothing could have prepared me for the metamorphosis I would experience after my son was born. I wasn't a guy who knew everything about the concept of children and their relationship to their parenthood, but I was well on my way to understanding it.

Looking back on my first job as a full-time youth minister, I really had no idea what the parents were experiencing. I loved the kids, but the overwhelming depth of emotion that you can feel when you hug your son or daughter is unimaginable. I could not empathize with them because I had no experience as a parent; but I do hope that I helped them to some degree despite my naïveté.

Bond With Your Children

I was equipped to love kids and to be a youth minister. I had the personality, the training, the experience, and was getting more training. Garbage. It is all garbage when compared to the bond formed between a parent and a child. I hope you are cultivating that bond.

The feeling I had when I saw my son for the first time? Curiosity. He was not yet 30 seconds old and was already trying to manipulate the system by crying. I felt concern for my wife. She had been through a lot; pregnancy is difficult on her tiny frame. She had some blood pressure issues, so my mind was with her. What didn't I feel? A bond that was immediate.

I felt pride too, but the depth of love that I have now did not immediately start then. Why? I didn't know him. I had to experience life with him before I became "Parent." This is why parenting is so difficult. No other job demands so much of a person, and there is no way you would go through diapers, sleepless nights, and worry over who she is dating to care nothing for this child.

The struggles are what bond us to our children. We have put too much into them to let them wander into the street or date a guy that can potentially ruin her future. This trial by fire commits us to the child we must ensure gets out of our house someday and makes it to eternity with us.

When my daughter was born, I understood "Parent" and bonded with her very quickly. My relationship with my son grows stronger every day as I work to shape him into a good man.

A Bond Forms

I could not be nor understand "Parent" because I had no reference point from which to draw. Once I received the much-needed experience, I could better empathize with parents I work with and even have a greater appreciation for my middle schoolers. I view them not simply as a concerned citizen but rather as an adult who knows their potential; their intrinsic value. My heart breaks when they are disappointed, and I feel the despair with a parent who is at the end of her rope. What if it were my child?

I was on a thirteen-mile hike one winter afternoon. We were in the South Cumberland State Park on the lower Stone Door trail. An easy trail until it is time to walk straight out of what is appropriately called, Savage Gulf. Halfway up this daunting trail, I had to sit down. Heaviest of the three (and apparently the most out of shape) I took out a banana and took a bite. Now, I have probably eaten dozens of bananas in my life, but this was by far the sweetest, best-tasting banana I had ever put in my mouth. This was not a special piece of fruit, but it was the difficulty of the journey that made it taste so good. It is the journey of a parent that causes us to bond and love our child so much. It is the journey that makes time with them so precious. It is through the suffering that we endure at the hand of a willful child and a world that wants their money, mind, and soul that we battle and grow into a relationship with our child that is unimaginable.

In the Old Testament, our heavenly Father experienced a lot with the children of Israel. They were with Him; they would leave Him; they would want to come back, and then the process would eventually start all over again. Each time God would deliver them through the work of a judge and the Israelites would fall again. Genesis 6 gives us a taste of what it was like for God when His creation departed from Him.

> "Then the Lord saw that the wickedness of man was great on the earth, and that every intent of the thoughts of his heart was only evil continually. The Lord was sorry that He had made man on the earth, and He was grieved in His heart" (verses 5 – 6).

When I was at that youth day in Bowling Green, something awoke inside of me. I had my nuclear family and I had my wife, both of which gave and received love freely. However, there was a part of me that wanted to do something else. Something different. It was at that moment that I had a desire to raise a child. To influence this child and make him into a great man (or woman) someday.

I believe this is God's plan for us. To awaken in each of us at some point a desire to raise a family. It is rewarding, but at the same time it is difficult much like God's relationship was with the children of Israel throughout their time in the wilderness. They would complain and He would supply. They would leave Him and He would give them up. They would suffer consequences and then return to Him acknowledging Him as their provider.

This similar experience that we have with our children forges us into the parents God would have us be, provided the experience does not drive us mad.

Radical Acceptance

While we are forming this deep bond with our children, we hope to learn what God means when He makes His promises to us, His children. I knew that I was a child of God, but I had no idea what that meant from His perspective. I had no idea what love for a child meant. What it meant to forgive a child when he does wrong. I couldn't comprehend what it meant to appreciate a child just for standing there and being mine. I was clueless of these concepts before I was a parent. Now, I can appreciate His love for me, and although not fully grasp its transcendent depth, I can imagine through my own world how He must feel about me. This is a great feeling.

This feeling helps me understand, at least to some degree, the level of acceptance offered to me by my heavenly Father. Marriage is emblematic of Christ's relationship with the church, and our parenting relationship resembles that with our own children. The sacrifice God made to give Jesus for our sins carries greater weight. No matter how much our children may mess up, we still love them and accept them.

Many will not notice this connection, and this is a great loss for them. They will not put the two together because they either have a weak relationship or no relationship with our heavenly Father. Parenting is a wonderful avenue to cultivate a Christian life, and see that we are truly loved by God and that we can be happy with nothing else but Him. Through parent workshops and lessons, we can grow stronger as a body of Christ and individually as we try to grasp the idea of Radical Acceptance.

Radical Acceptance is a term used to describe in our limited English vocabulary just what God can and will do for us. We understand acceptance, but there is always a limit as to how far someone will go with this. Teens are notorious for this. They have friends until they no longer serve a direct purpose for their selfish desires. We have our own limits as to how much we will accept ourselves. We feel guilt and personal hatred when we do wrong, but by saying "radical acceptance" we understand that this extends beyond what we would normally feel.

Jesus radically accepted those who were sinners, loathed by society, and even had deathly diseases such as leprosy. Where have you been with your sick child? A stomach virus? Your child is in your arms. A fever? Your child is in your arms. Breaking curfew? Your child is held in your arms because you are thankful they are safe.

Some struggle with becoming a Christian because "How could God ever love me?" or "How can God ever forgive all that I have done?" If they have children, they should look at their own. They should look at what they would be willing to do for that child and then realize that it is God who offers us the same type of love. Yet, His offering goes into eternity.

This understanding is provided when we fully grasp our role as a parent. I joke about being the ruler of my children's universe, but it is not far from the truth. Although I am not a god, of course, I do have a responsibility to ensure that all that they do will be good for them. I need to help them see the good in having a work ethic, in saying "no" to that which is bad, and to see that they are answerable to authority. These are lessons lost on many young people, but are exactly what will help them submit to a Christian life. As a side note, this level of authority needs to be established early on. Trying to do it with a fifteen-year-old will be difficult, to say the least. As your child grows, a lengthening of this proverbial leash is necessary to establish autonomy and the desire to do what is right out of love rather than fear. The second will not last.

Your child should see the value in listening to you. The Israelites no doubt saw how good they had it with God after they were over-taken by the Mesopotamians (Judges 3:8). Thinking they wanted something else, they would rebel against God, and God would allow them to be overtaken. Then the Israelites would return. A time may come when "tough love" is necessary with your child. As we look to our heavenly Father for an example, we know the value in a person. "But My people did not listen to My voice, and Israel did not obey Me. So I gave them over to the stubbornness of their heart, to walk in their own devices" (Psalm 81:11-12).

How often does your child beg to go somewhere, date someone, or do something you know will be no good for them? What happens between you and your teen when you are clearly divided on an important topic? Do you discipline maliciously until they submit? Do you talk to them calmly until you give in, or do you have some other method?

I'll tell you what does not work long-term is pure fear. It works short-term. You can get your child to stop doing something by being scary and causing them to huddle in a corner, but your child will never see the value in this method. He stopped hitting his sister or knows that what he did was wrong, but in no way are you growing the bond between the two of you. The only thing he may learn from the experience is that you can get loud.

I was at a business establishment in my town with my son. Another little boy had misbehaved and been reprimanded for his behavior by the teacher. As we were leaving, his siblings told their dad about the incident. As I passed their van, I watched as the little boy was screaming in the second seat. It was the kind of scream that comes only when a child is afraid. Dad was still outside the car but climbed into the back with the boy shrieking from fear. I watched, prepared to do something if necessary. (Being a counselor, I'm very comfortable with butting into people's lives). Thankfully, it was not as bad as I had worried. Maybe Dad held back his regular punishment that the boy expected, maybe he did something that I couldn't see, or maybe the little boy is just a drama queen. In any case, the boy was afraid of Dad because of fear. In the movie, *The Secret Life of Bees*, Dakota Fanning's character gets punished by kneeling down on a pile of dry grits. This is both painful and pointless.

"Those who hate the Lord would pretend obedience to Him, and their time *of punishment* would be forever" (Psalm 81:15). A child who is pointlessly and harshly punished does not see the value in consequences. They see only the parent who is needlessly cruel.

How can you make your child want to come back to you after administering consequences? It is not magic. With your child screaming in fear, why would he want to come back to you? How can he learn the value of listening to you? How can you enjoy your child after punishing him if the punishment does not fit the crime? When the two are not related, nothing is learned. When God disciplined the Israelites, He did so through the behavior they were already exhibiting. Because they were worshiping idols and marrying those from other lands, so He allowed them to go into what they wanted. When they were taken over by groups, God allowed them to see what happened when you leave Him. This is still the result of their behavior as He gave them protection as well. When the consequences were played out, they wanted to go back to God.

We must make the child feel good about his consequences because after the lesson is learned, appreciation is felt, not resentment. We must show love, not hatred, and convey compassion, not anger. Express concern, not apathy. Your child will not like the consequences, but there is a feeling that overcomes us when we do and experience good.

The Prodigal Father?

We see ourselves in the story of the prodigal son. We are either the lost son coming back for forgiveness or the bitter son resentful to his father for doing what he should have done in the first place.

The father let his son go because that is what he wanted. Your children will want this, and the day may come when you must comply because nothing else is working. Will you or have you let your child go? We know that listening to us is best for them, but they do not seem to get this. "Oh that My people would listen to Me, that Israel would walk in My ways! I would quickly subdue their enemies and turn My hand against their adversaries" (Psalm 81:13-14). The children of Israel didn't see this. It took harsh experience to make this lesson clear to them.

With everything you do right as a parent, your child is still an autonomous person with thoughts and a will of his own. When it comes right down to it, he must make the final decision as to whether he follows God.

I have spoken to parents who have done what they should have done. They were the youth workers, at worship every Sunday and praying at every meal. They were the ones whose children should still be faithful, but they are not. To these parents I say, even God loses children.

We are also the father, the parent in this story. Pleading with our child not to leave, we finally give in as we reach the end of our options. The son is going to leave with or without our help so we might as well help him. It gives him one less reason to "hate us for keeping him down and feeling like he is in a prison." Hurt by the actions of our child, we watch him leave, but then patiently wait as we know how this story plays out. While looking to the horizon, we see him coming. What do you do? Run to meet him as the father in the story does or is there bitterness in your heart? "You squandered my money? You ungrateful child!" If these are the types of messages the child received regularly, he probably won't be back, but if he knows you are always ready to forgive and accept him, then you keep a steady eye on the horizon. He will return.

Your Child's Spiritual Path

Some preachers and parents question the wisdom of baptizing a child who is eight, nine or ten years old. Can they grasp entirely what they are doing? I'm not sure we ever do totally, but if you take a child to church every Sunday and teach him about doing what is right and obeying God, what do we expect? As a child's brain develops in his early years, he lacks the capacity to think abstractly; outside of the world he can observe. A man who died for Him 2000 years ago is such a concept. Bible stories seem like tales on a foam board that do not really have a life of their own. What is not abstract is this: Follow Christ and you will be rewarded. Follow God by becoming a Christian. Do not be surprised if your young child wants to become a Christian. It is an obvious choice.

Later, a second change must occur as he becomes a teenager. He loses some of the traits that allow him to learn at an incredible rate. This change, some believe, makes room for the growth of the brain where abstract thinking occurs. His concerns change and the reason for becoming a Christian a few years earlier seem elementary. He must actually make a second decision as he is bombarded with messages that conflict with what he has been taught. He must decide if he is to be a prodigal or commit to Christ in this new life of a teen (and later an adult) where he finds himself.

Conclusion

Through your child's path, you must be there to guide them and pray that you are the parent God would have you to be. While raising your child, you must model much and work to shape them as a mentor but ensure that your guiding principles taken from scripture will raise a faithful Christian.

Are you raising your child to have your faith or is it his own? You want to pass your faith on to your child because hopefully you believe it to be good, true, and right. However, your child's faith must later become his own as this indicates a true conversion and a desire to follow our heavenly Father . . . their heavenly Father.

Questions for Discussion

1. How much time and in what ways have you spent with your child this week?

2. How does your experience as a parent help you with your experience as a Christian, realizing God's forgiveness and level of sacrifice?

3. Who are you in the story of the prodigal son?

ENDORSEMENTS

The family has always been the backbone of American Society. Dale Sadler has done an outstanding job in outlining powerful, practical & hopeful parenting suggestions for the next several generations. This timely book combines scripture, current research, and clinical insight to restore the family to it's happy and productive purpose for all family members and society. This book creates a rich tapestry of worthwhile reading for any parent. I recommend it highly.

> Mike Cravens, Ed.D,
> Director of M.S. Clinical Mental Health Counseling Program
> Freed-Hardeman University
> Henderson, TN. 38340

The great task of raising spiritually mature children can be daunting. Dale's book gives encouragement to parents through this journey by outlining their roles of modeling, mentoring, and guiding. These principles, if utilized, will benefit any family that reads this book.

> Michael Jones, Ed. S., LPC-S, NCC, DCC
> Professional Counselor in Private Practice
> Searcy, AK

Role confusion is creating cracks within the fabric of the American family. Dale Sadler's book provides a methodology to restore vitality to the home. Too often parents are providing a poor example, or are outsourcing parenting to the larger culture, instead of being mentor to their children. In his book, he provides practical wisdom to overcome the decline in parent-child relationships. This is the book that will give you the strength, skills, and insights to make a difference to those whom you dearly love.

> Matthew Morine, D.Min
> Pulpit Minister
> Castle Rock Church of Christ
> Castle Rock, CO

Generations to Come is a valuable contribution to the inspirational parenting literature.

John Conger, PhD. CFLE
Certified Family Life Educator and Family Social Scientist
Family & Consumer Sciences, College of Arts and Sciences
Lipscomb University

Dale Sadler's advice to parents comes from his experience as a dedicated counselor, father and husband. In his new book, *Generations to Come: Becoming All Things to Your Child*, Dale writes about the necessity of every parent becoming his or her child's "Model, Mentor and Guide," and explains how to fulfill those roles. I have no doubt readers will enjoy Dale's book, as they enjoy his blog posts on *EmpoweringParents.com*, and glean from his words many seeds of wisdom that they will be able to plant and nurture as their child grows.

Elisabeth Wilkins,
Editor, *EmpoweringParents.com*

Parenting is a difficult mission to navigate. In my experience as a pediatrician of 26 years, I have seen the deterioration of the family structure. Many more divorces are seen now, and families are under even more stress in this generation. Dale Sadler has incorporated his many years of experience as a family counselor and developed core guidelines of parenthood that even the best of parents can utilize. I am thrilled to see a book of this nature written. It is long overdue. I will wholeheartedly recommend this wonderful book to ALL of my families!

W. Stephen Johnson, M.D.